BEGINNERS ESL LESSON PLANS BOOK 1

Learning English Curriculum

Since 1999

www.efl-esl.com

Published by:
Learning English Curriculum

ISBN 9781772454086

Visit us on the Web at
https://www.efl-esl.com

Learning English Curriculum
Victoria, B.C. Canada
E-mail: **info@efl-esl.com**

About Learning English Curriculum Ltd.

Learning English Curriculum began in Czechoslovakia in 1990. Shortly after the Velvet Revolution that freed the country of Communism. The authors began writing these lessons as they taught English to their Czech Students at the English Centre in Karlovy Vary. The students played a vital role in the development of this series. The authors consulted with them by having them complete student surveys wherein they rated the extensive variety of activities and lessons that they had participated in. Discussion of the results followed and any item that was rated below 8, on a scale of 1 to 10, was discarded. Thus, Learning English Curriculum evolved through consultation with our English second language students.

Since 20095 thousands of people around the world have visited our web sites. At this time purchases of our Teen-Adult Curriculum, Children's Curriculum, Children's Storybooks and our listening programs have been made from more than 100 countries.

At Learning English Curriculum, we have a suggestion regarding the printing of our books in an economical and environmentally friendly way. It is our experience that when students begin something new there are always those that, for a number of reasons, don't continue. In order to cut expenses and avoid wasting paper, we suggest that you begin the classes by providing only the first lessons of the printed book. These small things do make a difference.

Customization of your covers

You may be interested in the customization of your covers. (White Label Services
This personalizes your textbooks and makes them a visible part of your school's curriculum. For this service contact us at: info@efl-esl.com

Members of our team with professional degrees have combined years of teaching experience and editing to produce these teaching materials.

Team Members for this publication:
Editors:
Daisy A. Stocker B.Ed., .Ed.
Dr. George A. Stocker D.D.S.

Contributor:
Brian Stocker MA

This book, Beginners Part 1 is dedicated to the people of Nepal, where we work with the Dalit people (untouchables) to improve their lives through education and financial aid.

During the past years we have been working with:

Bhupendra Ghimire
Founder President
Volunteers Initiative Nepal (VIN
EU AID Volunteers Initiative Certified Organization
Member of CCIVS, NVDA & ALLIANCE of European VSO
Sister Charities: Friends of VIN **Netherlands, USA, UK** and **Canada**
https://www.volunteersinitiativenepal.org/
e-mail: vinnepal@gmail.com
"Empowering the most marginalised communities"

WWe have greatly enjoyed working with the friendly, eager to learn, Nepalese people.
It has been a pleasure to provide English language materials for the Dalit people, who have suffered terrible discrimination for centuries.

Bhupendra Ghimire, Daisy and George Stocker with the teachers in Kathmnandu.

TEACHING PHILOSOPHY

Our teaching philosophy means that the students and teachers can combine fun and learning, while communicating in English. This is a structured approach, meaning that each new concept is mastered in a conversational English environment before another is introduced. During the past decade, research has shown that the students learn more effectively if the teaching of grammar is integrated with a communicative approach to the learning of the English language.

This program is written for students 13 years and older. We introduce the basic tenses and other structures in a logical sequence, integrating them with light hearted activities that provide practice in a conversational setting. The combination achieved in our curriculum has proved to be popular with the students and successful in achieving its goals.

TIMING AND LESSON STRUCTURE

The most successful order of presentation for the lessons is outlined below:
- Greeting the students in English
- Oral questions (20 to 30 minutes)

Oral Questions may be done before or after the new lesson has been introduced.
The order suggested in the Student's Book should be adapted to the needs of the group.
- Introduction of a new lesson or continuation of a past lesson.
- Completion of exercises and / or partner activities
- Ending with a more relaxed conversational activity

VOCABULARY

The new words introduced in each lesson are listed under the title and may be introduced in any of the following ways:
- The teacher may write the words on the blackboard and use them in sentences.
- The teacher can dramatize, draw or use the pictures to explain the words.
- The students can work in small groups with their dictionaries.

ORAL QUESTIONS

The oral questions are designed to provide practice in speaking.
The questions and answers stress grammatical structure, and word order of the English language.
When our students completed surveys where Oral Questions were rated "helpful / not helpful" on a scale of 1 to 10, **Oral Questions were consistently rated as "10 - very helpful".**
Teaching this Conversational English program without using the oral questions will result in the lessons becoming too difficult for the students.

These questions provide the basic models of the English Language.
They are a vital part of the program, giving practice, review and an opportunity for the teacher to expand the language to talk about local events.

TESTS

The tests are a part of the learning process. They allow the students to identify the areas they need to study. When marking the sentence answers, subtract one mark for each error.

-If a student has one mistake, he or she will get 3 marks for that answer
-If a student has two mistakes, he or she will get 2 marks for that answer
-If a student has three mistakes, he or she will get 1 mark for that answer
-If a student has four or more mistakes, he or she won't get any marks

GIVE SPECIAL ATTENTION TO INDIVIDUAL NEEDS WHEN MARKING

The teacher should use discretion when marking. Some students work very hard but have difficulty. They should be given the best possible mark. Some students learn easily but become careless, so they should be marked down for their mistakes. In other words, the teacher needs to be aware of the needs of the students. The tests are designed to make most of the students feel good about their English but also give a clear signal to those who aren't making satisfactory progress.

WHAT KIND OF MISTAKES SHOULD BE CONSIDERED?

Marks should be deducted for:
- not knowing the right vocabulary
- word order mistakes
- grammatical errors
- no marks are given if the student doesn't understand the question

Do **not** deduct marks for spelling mistakes if you can understand what the student means.
Students with marks above 80% are ready to continue with the program.
Test answers are included in the Guide.

ANSWERS TO THE ORAL TEST QUESTIONS

The teachers have the choice of having the students answer orally or in writing. As some of the teachers are speaking English as a second language, it might be difficult for them to test pronunciation. If the teacher can understand what the student is saying then the pronunciation should be accepted. Internationally, it is acceptable if the speaker is understood.

The tests are out of 50 except for the last test in Part 1 and in Part 2.
There are no absolutes when assessing test marks. Many factors always enter into the mark. These can range from the student being sick that day to some problem at home. It's also possible that the student missed a lot of classes due to illness.

The purpose of these tests is to allow the students to see where they are having difficulty. This lets them know where they should spend their time when they study.
This is the most important aspect of the tests.

ANSWERS

Answers in the Guide are written in italics. The suggested answers are the most likely, but others are possible.

GLOSSARY

The glossary contains the vocabulary.
The verbs are shown in the infinitive form: do (to.
The past tenses are included for reference in the glossary, shown as: infinitive, past tense.

CONTENTS   LESSONS 1-20

The English second language complete teaching curriculum includes four books. Each book has 20 lessons in Part 1 and 20 in Part 2. New concepts are incrementally introduced. Each lesson contains three books Student Reader, Student Workbook and Teacher's Guide.

The Table of Contents for each book shows new concepts, oral activities, written exercises and large and small group activities. Answers are included for all questions and discussions. Unit and final tests are provided throughout.

Beginners PART 1

	Student	Workbook	Guide
LESSON 1	1	1	1

Names
Vocabulary
Subject pronouns
To be
Written exercises
Oral questions
Whole class team activity

LESSON 2	2	2	4

Possessive adjectives
Vocabulary
Listening and answering
Role-play – large group in unison
Small group oral question and answer activities
Oral questions
Written exercises
Large group team activity

Printing Instructions

Student Reader   Pages 14 – 51
Student Workbook Pages 52 – 97
Teacher Guide   Pages 98 – 183

BEGINNERS ESL LESSONS
BOOK 1

STUDENT READER

Learning English
Curriculum
Since 1999
www.efl-esl.com

LESSON 1

Hello, I am _____. I am a teacher.

What is your name? _____ ?

My name is _____.

VOCABULARY:	what	yes	no	hello
my	your	name	student	teacher
dog	singular	plural	who	and
answer (to)	sentence	be (to)	a	friend

Singular (1)	TO BE	Plural (2+)
I am		we are
You are		you are
He is		they are
She is		
It is		

ACTIVITY 1: Listen to your teacher read the question.
Then you, the students, read the answer with the other students in the class.

Singular

What is your name?

Are you a student?

Is he a student?

Is she your friend?

Is it your dog?

What is your teacher's name?

My name is _____.

Yes, I am a student.

Yes, he is a student.

Yes, she is my friend.

Yes, it is my dog.

My teacher's name is _____.

Plural

Are we friends?

Are you students?

Are they student?

Are dogs friendly??

Yes, we are friends.

Yes, we are students.

Yes, they are students.

Yes, dogs are friendly.

ACTIVITY 3 – TEACHER'S GUIDE PAGE 3
EXERCISE 1 – WORKBOOK PAGE 1
ACTIVITY 2 – WORKBOOK PAGE 2

Student Reader

ORAL QUESTIONS TEACHER'S GUIDE

LESSON 2

ACTIVITY 1:   **Listen and repeat.**

VOCABULARY:

adjective	possessive	father	classmate	restaurant
class	in	this	mother	like (to)
have (to)	where	no	motorcycle	drive (to)
car	do (to)	outside	friendly	an

POSSESSIVE ADJECTIVES
Singular	Plural
my	our
your	your
his / her / its	their

ACTIVITY 2:   **Listen to your teacher ask each question. You read the answer orally.**

Are you in an English class?   Yes, I am in an English class.
Are you my friend? (Yes)   Yes, I am your friend.
Is he your classmate? (Yes)   Yes, he is my classmate.
Is a dog a friend? (Yes)   Yes, a dog is a friend.

Is this our English class?   Yes, this is our English class.
Are your friends in this class? (Yes)   Yes, my friends are in this class.
Are your friends' students? (Yes)   Yes, my friends are students.

ACTIVITY 3:   **Close your book. Listen to your teacher read the above questions again and answer without looking.**

ACTIVITY 4:   **Listen to the dialogue. Role-play it and then change roles.**

Raymond: Hello, my name is Raymond.
Nancy: Hello, I am Nancy.
Raymond: Do you like cars?
Nancy: Yes, I like cars.

Raymond: Do you have a car?
Nancy: Yes, I have a car.

Raymond: I have a motorcycle.

Nancy: I like motorcycles.

LESSON 2 CONTINUED

ACTIVITY 5: **The students should ask and answer the following questions.**

1. Does Nancy have a car??
2. Is her name Nancy??
3. Does Raymond have a motorcycle??
4. Does Nancy like motorcycles??
5. Do you like motorcycles??

6. What is your *friend's* name?
7. What is your *teacher's* name?
8. What is your *mother's* name?
9. What is your *father's* name?

10. Do you like cars?? (yes)
11. What is your name??
12. Do you like dogs?? (yes)
13. Do you have a motorcycle?? (yes)
14. Are you a student??
15. Do you drive a car?? (yes)
16. Do you like motorcycles?? (yes)
17. Do you like restaurants?? (yes)

1. Yes, Nancy has a car.
2. Yes, her name is Nancy.
3. Yes, Raymond has a motorcycle.
4. Yes, Nancy likes motorcycles.
5. Yes, I like motorcycles.

6. His / Her name is …
7. His / Her name is...
8. Her name is ...
9. His name is ...

10. Yes, I like cars.
11. My name is _____.
12. Yes, I like dogs.
13. Yes, I have a motorcycle.
14 Yes, I am a student.
15. Yes, I drive a car.
16. Yes, I like motorcycles.
17. Yes, I like restaurants.

ORAL QUESTIONS   TEACHER'S GUIDE

ACTIVITY 6:   **Role-play the dialogue together.**
Boys are Raymond - Girls are Nancy

TEACHER: Raymond and Nancy are on his motorcycle.

RAYMOND: I like to drive my motorcycle.

NANCY: I like motorcycles and dogs. Do you have a dog?

RAYMOND: Yes, I have a dog.

NANCY: Where is your dog?

RAYMOND: It is outside.

NANCY: Is it friendly?

RAYMOND: Yes, it is a friendly dog.

ACTIVITY 8: PAGE 6 TEACHER'S GUIDE

LESSON 2 CONTINUED

ACTIVITY 7: Divide into small groups. Ask and answer, then check your answers in the box.

1. What does Raymond like to do?

2. What does Nancy like?

3. Where is Raymond's dog?

4. Is his dog friendly?

5. Do you like friendly dogs? (yes)

6. Do you like to drive a motorcycle? (yes)

> 1. Raymond likes to drive his motorcycle.
>
> 2. Nancy likes motorcycles and dogs.
>
> 3. Raymond's dog is outside.
>
> 4. Yes, it is friendly.
>
> 5. Yes, I like friendly dogs.
>
> 6. Yes, I like to drive a motorcycle.

ACTIVITY 4: Divide into groups of two or three and ask each other these questions. Answer in sentences.

Are they friends?

_____

Does he have a motorcycle?

_____

Is this a car?

_____

Is this a dog?

_____

Is he a policeman?

_____

Is she a nurse?

_____

Student Reader

4

LESSON 3

ACTIVITY 1: Divide into four groups – two groups of boys – Tom and Peter.

Two groups of girls – Carol and Sarah
Teacher - Narrator
Role-play the dialogue several times, each group speaking in unison.
Then change roles.

Four friends are in a restaurant. They order a glass of Sprite.

WAITER / WAITRESS:	Hello! What do you want to order?
PETER:	We all want a glass of Sprite. Four glasses of Sprite, please.
WAITER / WAITRESS:	Good, four glasses of cold Sprite.
NARRATOR:	Here is your order.
TOM:	Thank you. It is good.
CAROL:	I like it cold.

LESSON 3 CONTINUED

NEGATIVE SENTENCES WITH "TO BE"

Put "not" after the verb "to be"

EXAMPLE:

Are you a student?
No, I <u>am not</u> a student.

Are they students?
No, they <u>are not</u> students.

Are you thirsty?
Yes, I am thirsty.

No, I <u>am not</u> thirsty.

ACTIVITY 2:   **Whole Class Activity**
Answer these questions in unison. Your answer will be **negative**.

1. Are you thirsty? (no)   No, I am not thirsty

2. Are you in a restaurant? (no)   No, I'm not in a restaurant.

3. Are you outside? (no)   No, I am not outside.

4. Is your mother in this English class? (no)   No, my mother is not in this English class.

5. Are your friends outside? (no)   No, my friends are not outside.

6. Are you hot? (no)   No, I am not hot.

EXERCISE 1 – WORKBOOK PAGE 4

ORAL QUESTIONS   TEACHER'S GUIDE

ACTIVITY 3:   **Divide into groups of two or three. Ask each other these questions.**

EXAMPLES: **Are you thirsty?**   Yes, I am thirsty.   **No, I am not thirsty.**
What do you like to order??
I like to order coffee.   **I like to order Sprite.**

1. Do you like cold drinks? (yes)

2. Do you like hamburgers? (yes)

3. Are you thirsty?

4. Do you like Sprite? (yes)

5. Are you outside?

6. Are you hot?

7. Do you like pizza? (yes)

8. Are you cold?

1 Yes, I like cold drinks.
2 Yes, I like hamburgers.
3 Yes, I am thirsty. / No, I am not thirsty.
4 Yes, I like Sprite
5 Yes, I am outside. / No, I am not outside.
6 Yes, I am hot. / No, I am not hot.
7 Yes, I like pizza.

EXERCISES 1 AND 2 – WORKBOOK – PAGE 4   **PICTURE BINGO PAGES 9-26 GUIDE**
ACTIVITY 4 AND EXERCISE 3 – WORKBOOK PAGE 5

LESSON 4

VOCABULARY:

girl	sister	juice	today
boy	brother	city	

CONTRACTIONS OF "TO BE"

Singular (1)	Plural (2+)
I am = I'm you	we are = we're
are = you're he	you are = you're
is = he's she is =	they are = they're
she's it is = it's	

ACTIVITY 1: Listen to your teacher ask each question and read the answer in unison.

Am I your teacher?	Yes, **you're** my teacher. No,
Are you a teacher?	**I'm** not a teacher. Yes, **she's**
Is she your friend? **Are**	my friend. Yes, **they're**
they students?	students. Yes, **he's** my
Is he your friend?	friend.
Are we in English class?	Yes, **we're** in English class.
Is it hot today?	Yes, **it's** hot today.
Are you a student?	Yes, **I'm** a student.

Now close your books and answer each question as your teacher asks it.

To form the negative of **"to do"**, put **"not"** after the verb or use the contraction.

Singular		**Plural**	
I do	I do not = I don't you	**we do**	we do not = we don't
you do	do not = you don't	**you do**	you do not = we don't
he does	he does not = he doesn't	**they do**	they do not = don't
she does	she does not = she doesn't		
it does	it does not = it doesn't		

EXERCISE 1 – WORKBOOK – PAGE 6

Read these questions and answers with your teacher.

Do you **have** friends?   Yes, **I have** friends.   No, I **don't have** friends.

Does a dog **like** pasta?   Yes, a dog **likes**   No, a dog **doesn't like pasta.**

pasta. **Does** he **drink** juice?   Yes, he **drinks**   No, he **doesn't drink** juice.

juice.

EXERCISE 2 – WORKBOOK – PAGE 6

ACTIVITY 2 – GUIDE PAGE 28

ORAL QUESTIONS   TEACHER'S GUIDE

7

Student Reader

LESSON 5

VOCABULARY:				
apple	meet (to)	mango	man	make (to)
noun	pasta	nice	sit (to)	pen
whose	six	mistake	eat (to)	chicken
pronoun	verb	correct (to)	bring (to)	write (to)

ACTIVITY 1: **Listen to your teacher read the paragraph below then read it in unison.**

Now each student is to read one sentence orally

Carol, Tom, Peter and Sarah are friends.
They order something in a restaurant.
Carol orders pasta.
Tom doesn't like pasta. He orders a hamburger.
Carol doesn't like apple juice.
Sarah doesn't like hamburgers. She orders chicken.
Peter orders pizza.
They all order mango juice.

EXERCISE 1 – WORKBOOK PAGE 7

ORAL QUESTIONS   TEACHER'S GUIDE   8

LESSON 5 CONTINUED

ACTIVITY 2: Divide into five groups to role-play the dialogue. Change roles.

NARRATOR: Your friends are in a restaurant.
The waiter makes mistakes.
The friends correct his mistakes.

Carol: Tom, is this your hamburger?

Tom: Yes, thanks, Carol.

Peter: Whose chicken is this?

Sarah: It's my chicken. Thanks Peter.

Tom: Whose pasta is this?

Carol: It's mine. I like pasta.

Sarah: Whose pizza is this?

Peter: It's mine. I like pizza.

EXERCISE 2: - WORKBOOK PAGE 7

VERBS
These are regular verbs.

singular	plural	singular	plural
to bring –		**to meet –**	
I bring	we bring	I meet	we meet
you bring	you bring	you meet	you meet
he brings	they bring	**he meets**	they meet
she brings		**she meets**	
it brings		**it meets**	
to make –		**to eat -**	
I make	we make	I eat	we eat
you make	you make	you eat	you eat
he makes	they make	**he eats**	they eat
she makes		**she eats**	
it makes		**it eats**	

1. Yes, I eat hamburgers.
   No, I don't eat hamburgers.

2. Yes, he/she eats hamburgers. No, he/she doesn't eat hamburgers.

3. No, I don't bring a dog to class.

4. No, he/she doesn't bring a dog to class.

5. Yes, I meet my brother.
   No, I don't meet my brother.

6. Yes, he/she meets her brother
   No, he/she doesn't meet…

7. Yes, I make hamburgers.
   No, I don't make hamburgers.

8. Yes, he/she makes pasta.
   No, he/she doesn't make…

ACTIVITY 3: Divide into groups of 3 or 4.
Ask these questions and answer in sentences:

1. Do you eat hamburgers?

2. Does **he/she** eat hamburgers?

3. Do you bring a dog to class?

4. Does **he/she** bring a dog to class?

5. Do you meet your brother?

6. Does **he/she** meet her brother?

7. Do you make hamburgers?

8. Does **he/she** make pasta?

LESSON 5 CONTINUED

INFORMAL INTRODUCTIONS

A lady is introducing Raymond and Peter.

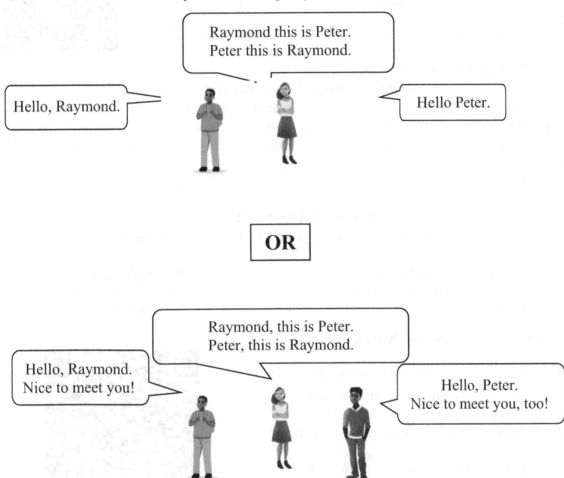

OR

ACTIVITY 4:

Give the students a name from the list below and divide them into groups of three.
One student is to introduce the other two. Then they should change roles.
Encourage them to move about the room introducing others in the class.

BOYS		GIRLS	
BRUCE	DANIEL	KATE	SUSAN
PETER	ROBERT	NANCY	MARY
DAVID	MARK	MARGARET	HELEN
BILL	JOHN	RITA	CAROL
ANDREW	TOM	SARAH	MARIA
LUKE	RAYMOND	ROSE	RUTH

EXERCISES 3 AND 4: - WORKBOOK PAGE 8

LESSON 6

VOCABULARY:	t-shirt	girl	great
last	full	town	buy (to)
surname	city	first	
middle	how about…?	study(to)	time
number	come (to)	new	picture

EXERCISE 1 – WORKBOOK PAGE 9

Negative contractions of the verb "to be".

I am   I am not = I'm not   **we are**   we are not = we're not = we aren't

you are   you are not = you're not = you aren't   **you are** you are not = you're not = you aren't

he is   he is not = he's not = he isn't   **they are** they are not = they're not = they aren't

she is   she is not = she's not = she isn't

it is   it is not = it's not = it isn't

ACTIVITY 1:   WHOLE CLASS ACTIVITY

Answer these questions orally using negative contractions of "to be".

1. Are you in a restaurant? (no)
2. Is she an American? (no)
3. Is he English? (no)
4. Are they waiters? (no)
5. Are we in Russia? (no)
6. Is he in town? (no)

EXERCISES 2 AND 3 – WORKBOOK PAGE 9

ACTIVITY 2:   Read this paragraph orally.

Divide into groups of three or four.
Ask each other the questions.
Try to answer, then look at the answers in the box.

Emily's name is Emily Jane Prescott.
Her first name is Emily.
Her middle name is Jane and her last name (surname) is Prescott.
Her full name is Emily Jane Prescott.

1. Is Emily a girl?

2. What is her first name?

3. What is her middle name?

4. What is her last name?

5. Is her surname "Prescott?"

6. What is her full name?

| 1. Yes, Emily is a girl. |
| 2. Her first name is Emily. |
| 3. Her middle name is Jane. |
| 4. Her last name is Prescott. |
| 5. Yes, her surname is Prescott. |
| 6. Her full name is Emily Jane Prescott. |

EXERCISE 4 – WORKBOOK PAGE 10

LESSON 6 CONTINUED

ORAL QUESTIONS   TEACHER'S GUIDE

ACTIVITY 3:   Read this paragraph. Divide into groups of two or three.
Ask each other the questions.
Try to answer, then look at the answers in the box.

David is a student. He studies English.
His friend Susan is a student.
She studies English too.

1.   Is David a teacher?

2.   What does he study?

3.   Who is David's friend?

4.   Is she a student?

5.   What does she study?

1. No, David isn't a teacher. David is a student.
2. He studies English.
3. Susan is David's friend.
4. Yes, she is a student.
5. She studies English.

EXERCISE 5 – WORKBOOK PAGE 10

INFORMAL INTRODUCTIONS
Self-introductions
They meet for the first time.

I'm Ruth.

Hi, Raymond.

Nice to meet you!

I'm Raymond.

Hello, Ruth.

Nice to meet you, too!

ACTIVITY 4 – SEE INSTRUCTIONS IN STUDENT READER PAGE 10

BOYS		GIRLS	
BRUCE	TOM	KATE	SUSAN
PETER	ROBERT	NANCY	MARY
DAVID	MARK	MARGARET	HELEN
BILL	JOHN	CAROL	CAROL
ANDREW	TOM	SARAH	MARIA

LESSON 6 CONTINUED

NEW VERB - TO COME

singular	plural
I come	we come
you come	you come
he comes	they come
she comes	
it comes	

ACTIVITY 5:   **ROLE-PLAY**

Divide into groups of five.
Listen to the dialogue and role-play it three or four times, changing roles.

Tom: I want to buy a new jacket.

Do you want to come?

Carol: Okay, I want to buy a T-shirt.

Narrator:

They walk to town.
Tom meets a friend.

Tom: Hello Bruce.

Bruce: Hi Tom. This is Margaret.

jacket

Tom: Nice to meet you, Margaret.

Carol: Hello, I'm Carol.

Bruce and Margaret: Hi, nice to meet you.

Carol: How about going to a restaurant?

Tom: Great! The Sunshine Restaurant is good.

Bruce and Margaret: See you there at 12:00.

LESSON 7

VOCABULARY:

sometimes	lady	how	family
fine	learn(to)	tea	history
go (to)	from	please (to)	formal
good-bye	son	daughter	

ACTIVITY 1:   **Look at the pictures.**
Ask your friends: **"What is _it_?"**
Your friend answers: **"_It_ is a ___".**

VOCABULARY

one – window	two – shoe	three – blouse	four – bird
five – jacket	six – tie	seven – hat	eight door
nine – house	ten – cat	eleven – cup of tea	twelve – T-shirt

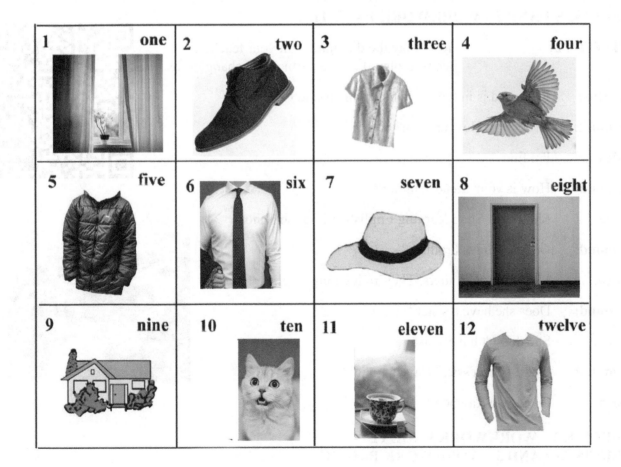

LESSON 7 CONTINUED

LET US INTRODUCE THE CARTER FAMILY:

Listen to your teacher read the paragraph below.
Then read it orally several times.

Craig and Jessica Carter are the father and mother.
Raymond Carter is their son and Ruth Carter is their daughter.
Their dog is Toto.

EXERCISES 1 AND 2 – WORKWORK PAGE 11

ACTIVITY 2: Role-play the dialogue with your teacher.
Then role-play it with a partner and change roles.

Narrator: Raymond is in town. He meets his friend George.

Raymond: Hi Jessica. How are you?

Jessica: I'm fine.

Raymond: How is your friend Jennifer?

Jessica: She's fine. She's learning English at English School.

Raymond: Does she have brothers?

Jessica: She has two brothers. They're learning English, too.

Raymond: Does she have a sister?

Jessica: She doesn't have a sister.

Raymond: Good-bye, Jessica. Have a good day.

Jessica: Good-bye Raymond.

EXERCISE 3 – WORKWORK PAGE 11
EXERCISES 4 AND 5 - WORKWORK PAGE 12

ORAL QUESTIONS   TEACHER'S GUIDE

LESSON 7 CONTINUED

IDIOM:

How do you do?
This is always used in formal introductions.

FORMAL INTRODUCTIONS
To the teacher:
Due to the COVID19 epidemic, Jessica and John are not shaking hands as is done in Western culture. Hand shaking may or may not return in the future.

ACTIVITY 3:
A lady is introducing Mary and John.
They are meeting for the first time.

Jessica, I'd like you to meet John.
John, this is Jessica.

How do you do, John?
I'm pleased to meet you.

How do you do, Jessica?
I'm pleased to meet you, too!

ACTIVITY 4:
The students are to take a name from the list below.
Divide into groups of three. One student introduces the other two.
Change roles.

BOYS		GIRLS	
BRUCE	DANIEL	KATE	SUSAN
PETER	ROBERT	NANCY	MARY
DAVID	MARK	MARGARET	HELEN
BILL	JOHN	RITA	CAROL
ANDREW	TOM	SARAH	MARIA
GEORGE		JENNIFER	

EXERCISES 6 AND 7 - WORKWORK PAGE 13
ACTIVITY 5 – GUIDE PAGE 38

LESSON 8 REVIEW

VOCABULARY:	live (to)	people	pen

ORAL QUESTIONS TEACHER'S GUIDE

EXERCISE 1 – WORKBOOK PAGE 14

ACTIVITY 1: **WHOLE CLASS ACTIVITY.**
Divide into two groups. Ask each other the question and answer in sentences.

1. Are you an English student?
2. Is this your book?
3. Does your house have a window?
4. Do you have a daughter?
5. What is your first name?
6. Does your mother have a dog?
7. Do you study English?

8. What is your surname?
9. Do you have a friend?
10. Are you in your house?
11. Does your father have a son?
12. What is your friend's name?
13. Does your father have a tie?
14. What is your last name?

EXERCISE 2 – WORKBOOK PAGE 15

ACTIVITY 2: **Divide into small groups. Ask these questions then look at the answers.**

1. Does your friend study English?

2. Does your mother live in Paris?

3. Do you live in Paris?

4. Is Paris in France?

5. Do you walk to English class?

6. Do you have four people in your fami

7. Is Mary a boy's name?

8. Is Tom a girl's name?

1. Yes, my friend studies English. No, my friend doesn't study English.

2. Yes, my mother lives in Paris. No, my mother doesn't live in Paris.

3. Yes, I live in Paris. No, I don't live in Paris.

4. Yes, Paris is in France.

5. Yes, I walk to English class. No, I don't walk to English class.

6. Yes, I have four people in my family. No, I don't have four people in my family. I have _____ people in my family.

7. No, Mary isn't a boy's name.

8. No, Tom isn't a girl's name.

ACTIVITY 3:

FIND A PARTNER ASK YOUR PARTNER   ANSWER IN SENTENCES:

EXAMPLE: <u>Do</u> you have a dog?   Yes, I have a dog.   No, I don't have a dog.

1. Do you have five sisters?
2. Do you have a son?
3. Do you meet your friend in town?
4. Do you like hamburgers?
5. Do you study French?

7. Do you eat pizza?
8. Do you have a hat?
9. Do you walk in town?
10. Do you live in a town?
11. Do you live in Canada?
12. Do you have a daughter?

TEST 2 TEACHER'S GUIDE PAGE 42

LESSON 9

NEGATIVE CONTRACTIONS
Contractions are a short way of speaking and writing.
The apostrophe (') shows where the letters are omitted.

Singular

to have

Plural

I have	I don't have
you have	you don't have
he has	he doesn't have
she has	she doesn't have
it has it	it doesn't have

we have	we don't have
you have	you don't have
they have	they don't have

ACTIVITY 1:   The students are to point to another student as they ask these questions.

Divide into small groups. Ask and answer these questions, then look at the answers.

1.   Does he have a cat? (no)

2.   Do they have hats? (no)

3.   Does she have a cup? (no)

4.   Do they have a bird? (no)

5.   Does he have a cup of tea? (no)

6.   Do they have a hamburger? (no)

7.   Does she have a glass of juice? (no)

8.   Do we have a chicken? (no)

9.   Do I have a picture of your town? (no)

1. No, he doesn't have a cat.
2. No, they don't have hats.
3. No, she doesn't have a cup.
4. No, they don't have a bird.
5. No, he doesn't have a cup of tea.
6. No, they don't have a hamburger.
7. No, she doesn't have a glass of juice.
8. No, we don't have a chicken
9. No, I don't have a picture of your town.

EXERCISE 1 – WORKBOOK PAGE 16
EXERCISE 2 – WORKBOOK PAGE 16

ORAL QUESTIONS   TEACHER'S GUIDE

LESSON 9 CONTINUED

POSSESSIVES:
Possessives also use an apostrophe (') to express possession.

EXAMPLES: grandfather's name   Mark's father   his sister's book

EXERCISE 3 - WORKBOOK PAGE 17
EXERCISE 4 - WORKBOOK PAGE 17

NEW VERBS

to say			to need		
Singular	**Plural**		**Singular**	**Plural**	
I say	we say		I need	we need	
you say	you say		you need	you need	
he says	they say		he needs	they need	
she says			she needs		
it says			it needs		

ACTIVITY 2:
Read the dialogue with your teacher. Then divide into groups of five.
Role-play the dialogue then change roles.

Narrator: Susan and John are friends. She goes to John's house to meet his grandparents.

John: Susan, I'd like you to meet my grandparents, Mr. and Mrs. Johnson.

Susan: How do you do, Mr. Johnson. (They shake hands) I'm pleased to meet you.

Grandfather: How do you do, Susan. I'm pleased to meet you, too.

Susan: How do you do, Mrs. Johnson. (They shake hands)

Grandmother: How do you do, Susan. I'm pleased to meet you.

Narrator: They all sit down.

Grandfather: I need a cup of tea. Do you like tea, Susan?

Susan: Yes, thank you.

Grandfather: You like tea, don't you John?

John: Thanks, I like tea.

Grandmother: I'm hot. I need a cold drink. I'd like mango juice.

Narrator: They all have something to drink.

ACTIVITY 3 – WORKBOOK PAGE 18
EXERCISE 5 - WORKBOOK PAGE 18

Student Reader

LESSON 10

A REFERENCE LIST OF COUNTRIES AND NATIONALITIES

VOCABULARY:

list	find (to)	partner	notebook	preposition
city	country	nationality		

Find the countries that are close to where you live.

If you can't see your country, print it on one of the lines below.

COUNTRY	NATIONALITY	COUNTRY	NATIONALITY
Afghanistan	Afghan	Iraq	Iraqi
Argentina	Argentinean	Italy	Italian
Australia	Australian	Ireland	Irish
Austria	Austrian	Japan	Japanese
Belgium	Belgian	Korea	Korean
Bolivia	Bolivian	Mexico	Mexican
Brazil	Brazilian	Nepal	Nepalese
Burma (Myanmar)	Burmese	Norway	Norwegian
Britain	British	Pakistan	Pakistani
Canada	Canadian	Peru	Peruvian
Chile	Chilean	Portugal	Portuguese
China	Chinese	Puerto Rico	Puerto Rican
Colombia	Colombian	Russia	Russian
Cuba	Cuban	Serbia	Serbian
Ecuador	Ecuadorian	South Africa	South African
England	English	Spain	Spanish
France	French	Sumatra	Sumatran
Denmark	Danish	Sweden	Swedish
El Salvador	Salvadorean	Switzerland	Swiss
Germany	German	Thailand	Thai
Greece	Greek	Tibet	Tibetan
Guatemala	Guatemalan	Turkey	Turkish
Holland (Netherlands)	Dutch	Ukraine	Ukrainian
India	Indian	United States	American
Vietnam	Vietnamese		

ACTIVITY 2 – WORKBOOK PAGE 19

LESSON 10 CONTINUED

GRAMMAR
The preposition "in" is used for countries and cities.

EXAMPLE: We live in <u>Canada</u>. We live <u>in</u> Vancouver.

"Do" is often used as a question word.

EXAMPLE: <u>Do</u> you live in Canada??
Yes, I live in Canada.
No, I do not (don't) live in Canada.

The third person singular in questions and the negative:
HE / SHE / IT

The verb "to do" always agrees with the subject.
The main verb takes its root form in a question and in the negative.

EXAMPLES: ***Does*** she live in Canada?   ***Does*** he have a book?
Yes, she ***lives*** in Canada.   Yes, he ***has*** a book.
No, she ***doesn't live*** in Canada.   No, he ***doesn't have*** a book.

ORAL QUESTIONS   TEACHER'S GUIDE

ACTIVITY 1:
Divide into small groups. Ask and answer these questions. Then look at the answers.

1. Does it have a T-shirt?

2. Does he have a hat?

3. Does she have a jacket?

4. Does he have a tie?

5. Does it have a hand?

6. Do they have glasses of juice?

1. No, it doesn' t have a T-shirt.
2. No, he doesn' t have a hat.
3. No, she doesn' t have a jacket.
4. No, he doesn' t have a tie.
5. No, it doesn' t have a hand.
6. No, they don' t have glasses of juice.

ACTIVITY 2 AND 3 – WORKBOOK PAGE 19
EXERCISE 1 AND 2 – WORKBOOK PAGE 20

LESSON 11

VOCABULARY:	How are things going? (This is an idiom)			
ask (to)	give (to)	at home	well	very
bad	sick	room	Hi	just
can	so-so	for	week	

ACTIVITY 1:   **GREETINGS:**

Role-play the dialogue with your teacher and then role-play it with a partner.

Bill meets his friend, Mary:

BILL: Hi, Mary, how are you?

MARY: Hi Bill, I'm fine, thank you. How are things going?

BILL: Things are going well.

REFERENCES FOR "GOOD"

How are you?   I'm fine, thank you.

                                                I'm fine, thanks.

How are things going?   Things are going well.

                                                I'm doing fine.

How are you doing?   Just great!

REFERENCES FOR "NOT GOOD"

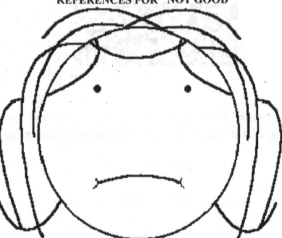

How are you?   I'm so-so.
                                                I'm not so good.
                                                I'm not very well.

How are things going?   Not badly.

                                                Not so good.

How are you doing?   I'm okay.

LESSON 11

EXERCISES 1, 2 AND 3 – PAGE 21
ACTIVITY 2:

Read the dialogue with your teacher.
Find a partner.
Role-play it.
Change roles.

Jane meets her friend Harry.

JANE:	Hi, Harry. How are you?
HARRY:	Hi, Jane. I'm not so good. This is a bad week. How are you doing?
JANE:	Just great.! Are you sick?
HARRY:	Yes, I'm at home from school today.
JANE:	You can have my notebook.
HARRY:	Thanks Jane.

ACTIVITY 3:

1. Is Jane a girl?

2. Is Harry a girl?

3. How is Harry?

4. Who is at home from school?

5. What does Jane give to Harry?

6. What does Harry say?

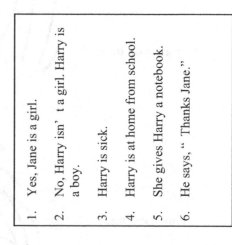

1. Yes, Jane is a girl.

2. No, Harry isn't a girl. Harry is a boy.

3. Harry is sick.

4. Harry is at home from school.

5. She gives Harry a notebook.

6. He says, " Thanks Jane."

ACTIVITY 4: The students are to move around the room asking each other these questions.
They can refer to Page 21 for some answers. Encourage them to try different answers.

1. How are you?

2. How are things going?

3. How are you doing?

EXERCISES 4 AND 5 – WORKBOOK PAGE 22

ACTIVITY 5:   **FIND A PARTNER: ASK THESE QUESTIONS**

1 How are things going?

2. How is your friend doing?

3. How are you?

4. How is your English going?

5. How are you doing with your English?

ACTIVITY 6: Divide the class into two groups - Student 1 and Student 2. The students pick a name, city and country from below, and move about the room role-playing the dialogue. They will need to find their nationality on Page 19.

Student 1:   Hi, I'm _____.
Student 2:   Hello, I'm _____.
Student 1:   Where are you from??
Student 2:   I'm from _____. I'm _____. (nationality)
             Where are you from??
Student 1:   I'm from _____. It's nice to meet you.
Student 2:   It's nice to meet you, too. Good-bye.
Student 1:   Good-bye.

KATE London, England	**HELENE** Paris, France	**BRUCE** Hong Kong, China
RITA Vancouver, Canada	**BILL** Dharmsala, India	**DANIEL** Frankfurt, Germany
JANE Budapest, Hungary	**ANDREW** New York, United States	**ROBERT** Moscow, Russia
MARIA Madrid, Spain	**HARRY** New York, United States	**MARY** Prague, Czech Republic
MARK Warsaw, Poland	**CAROL** Vancouver, Canada	**NANCY** Delhi, India

ACTIVITY 7 – GUIDE PAGES 49 AND 50

Student Reader

LESSON 12   REVIEW

VOCABULARY:	their	usually	wear (to)	dress

ACTIVITY 1:   **1. Read the questions with your teacher.**
                         2. Work with a partner, ask and answer the questions orally in sentences.

PICTURE 1 Mary John

1.   Are they meeting? (Yes)   _____

2.   Are they shaking hands?   _____

3.   Do you usually shake hands?   _____

4.   What do they say when they shake hands?   _____

5.   Does she wear a dress?   _____

6.   Do they have shoes?   _____

PICTURE 2

7.   Is Toto a cat?   _____

8.   Is your last name Carter?   _____

9.   Do they have a dog?   _____

10.   Does Ruth have a sister?   _____

11.   Does Craig have a son?   _____

12.   Does Ruth have a son?   _____

13.   Are they a family?   _____

14.   Is Toto their dog?   _____

Craig   Jessica   Raymond Ruth

PICTURE 3

15.   Does she have a T-shirt?   _____

16.   Does she talk to him?   _____

17.   Does she wear a dress?   _____

18.   Does he have a hat?   _____

EXERCISE 1 – WORKBOOK PAGE 23
EXERCISE 2 – WORKBOOK PAGE 24
EXERCISE 3 – WORKBOOK PAGE 25
TEST 3-GUIDE PAGES 53-54

LESSON 13

ACTIVITY 1:

Repeat each number and word after your teacher.

1 one — hospital	**2** two — watch	**3** three — mountains	**4** four
5 five — glass	**6** six — motorcycle	**7** seven — plate	**8** eight — theatre
9 nine — face	**10** ten — dress	**11** eleven	**12** twelve
13 thirteen — bridge	**14** fourteen — match	**15** fifteen — box	**16** sixteen — walet
17 seventeen — desk	**18** eighteen — pencil	**19** nineteen — toy	**20** twenty — page

LESSON 13 CONTINUED

ACTIVITY 2: **Listen and repeat the numbers with your teacher.**

0-zero	twenty-two	twenty-six
ten	twenty-three	twenty-seven
twenty	twenty-four	twenty-eight
twenty-one	twenty-five	twenty-nine
thirty	sixty	ninety
forty	seventy	one hundred
fifty	eighty	

ORAL QUESTIONS   TEACHER'S GUIDE

SINGULAR AND PLURAL

To form the plural of most nouns: add <u>s</u>.

EXAMPLE: singular - boy   **plural - boys**   **Here are two boys.**

If the nouns end in <u>sh</u>, <u>ch</u>, <u>s</u>, <u>z</u>, or <u>x</u>, add -<u>es</u>.

dish - **dish<u>es</u>**   watch – **watch<u>es</u>**   **box – box<u>es</u>**   **Dress - dress<u>es</u>.**

When nouns end in y:
When the y is preceded by a vowel - add <u>s</u>: boy - boy<u>s</u>
When the y is preceded by a consonant - change the <u>y</u> to <u>i</u> and add <u>es</u>.

dictionary – **dictionar<u>ies</u>**   activity – **activit<u>ies</u>**   city - **cit<u>ies</u>**

EXERCISE 1 – WORKBOOK PAGE 26
EXERCISE 2– WORKBOOK PAGE 26
EXERCISE 3– WORKBOOK PAGE 26

LESSON 13 CONTINUED

ACTIVITY 3:   **Introduce this activity with the whole class.**
Then they are to work in groups of two or three.
ASK YOUR PARTNER.   **(Do not use the negative.)**
The students are to choose any number from 1 to 20 for each item.
NOTE: a may be used instead of one.

EXAMPLE: **How many watches do you have?**
I have (one / a) watch.   **I have seventeen watches.**

How many rings do you have?   How many wallets do you have?
How many pencils do you have?   How many books do you have?
How many dictionaries do you have?   How many matches do you have?
How many pens do you have?   How many boxes do you have?
How many toys do you have?   How many dishes do you have?

EXERCISE 4 – WORKBOOK PAGE 27
EXERCISE 5 – WORKBOOK PAGE 27

ACTIVITY 4:   **This is a whole class activity.**

**The teacher and the students are to find the following objects and place them on the desks
in front of any of the students:
matches, wallet, toy, dish, pens, pencils, box.
The other items necessary for this activity will be visible on the desks or on the students.
The students are to answer the following questions in sentences.**

EXAMPLE: **Who has a toy?**   **DANIEL has a toy.**
1. Who has a watch?   8. Who has a ring?
2. Who has a wallet?   9. What has pages?
3. Who has a dictionary?   10. Who has glasses?
4. How many teachers are here?   11. Who has a box? (No one has a box.)
5. Who has a pencil?   12. Who has a box of matches?
6. Who has a book?   13. Who has a dish? (No one has a dish.)
7. Who has a dress?   14. Who is a boy?

desk

matches

ACTIVITY7 - GUIDE PAGE 58

LESSON 14

VOCABULARY:

speak (to)	see (to)	read (to)
some	any	idea

CONTRACTIONS OF AUXILIARY VERBS WITH NOT:

is not = isn't	do not = don't
are not = aren't	does not = doesn't
have not = haven't	has not = hasn't

USING THE NEGATIVE:
"Not" expresses a negative idea:

Auxiliary verb + not + main verb
He   does + not + read.

Do or **does** is used with **not** to make a present tense verb negative.
I <u>do not</u> go.   He <u>does not</u> go.
I <u>don't</u> go.   He <u>doesn't</u> go.

Using "do" in <u>questions</u> and in <u>negative</u> sentences.
EXAMPLE: <u>Do</u> you have a pen?
No, I <u>do not (don't)</u> have a pen.
Yes, I have a pen.

EXERCISES 1 AND 2 - WORKBOOK PAGE 28

Using "SOME" and "ANY"   EXAMPLES:
Use "some" in questions and positive sentence

> Do they have <u>some</u> motorcycles?
>
> Yes, they have <u>some</u> motorcycles.

Use "any" in negative sentences.

> Do they have some motorcycles?
>
> They don't have any motorcycles.

WORKBOOK PAGE 28
ACTIVITY 2 – WORKBOOK PAGE 29
EXERCISE 3 – WORKBOOK PAGE 30
ACTIVITIES 3 AND 4 – GUIDE PAGES 61 AND 62

ORAL QUESTIONS   TEACHER'S GUIDE

LESSON 15

VOCABULARY: men – women (plural)   man – woman (singular)

white	apple	glasses	handle
red	umbrella	big	one (pronoun)
specific	brown	football	theater
here's [here is]	look for (to)		

PRONOUNS

Do   you   see   <u>Bob</u>?   Yes,   I   see   <u>him</u>.
(subject) (verb) (object)   (subject) (verb) (object)

SUBJECT PRONOUNS

IMPERSONAL PRONOUNS
I   one   me

OBJECT PRONOUNS

you
he, she, it
we
you
they

"one" can be used as a subject pronoun
or an object pronoun.

One can help others. (formal)
They all helped to find the lost <u>one</u>.

you
him, her, it
us
you
them

EXERCISE 1 – WORKBOOK PAGE 31

USE <u>A</u> OR <u>THE</u> BEFORE ALL <u>SINGULAR</u> NOUNS.

> **USING <u>A</u> AND <u>AN</u>**
> Use "<u>a</u>" before all consonants. I have <u>a</u> wallet.

> Use <u>an</u> before nouns starting with (a,e,i,o,u)
> She has <u>an</u> umbrella.

> **USING THE:** I like **the** big apple.
> (It is one specific apple.)

EXERCISE 2 – WORKBOOK PAGE 31

ORAL QUESTIONS   TEACHER'S GUIDE

LESSON 15 CONTINUED

ACTIVITY 1:

Divide into small groups and ask each other these questions.

NOTE:

Man and woman are singular. They both have an "a".
Men and women are plural. They both have an "e".

1. Is <u>wallets</u> a singular noun?

2. Is <u>dictionary</u> a singular noun?

3. Is <u>men</u> a singular noun?

4. Is <u>man</u> a singular noun?

5. Is <u>women</u> a plural noun?

6. Is <u>woman</u> a singular noun?

7. Is Jane a boy?

8. Is Martin a boy?

9. Do you have a basketball?

10. Do you have a soccer ball?

1. No, <u>wallets</u> isn't a singular noun.

2. Yes, <u>dictionary</u> is a singular noun.

3. No, <u>men</u> isn't a singular noun.

4. Yes, <u>man</u> is a singular noun.

5. Yes, <u>women</u> is a plural noun.

6. Yes, <u>woman</u> is a singular noun.

7. No, Jane isn't a boy.

8. Yes, Martin is a boy.

9. Yes, I have a basketball.
   No, I don't have a basketball.

10. Yes, I have a soccer ball.
    No, I don't have a soccer ball.

ACTIVITY 2

Divide into groups of three, listen to the dialogue and role-play it. Then change roles.

Narrator: Jane has her basketball.
Martin has his soccer ball.

Jane: I love basketball.

Martin: I like soccer.

Jane: I have a new basketball.

Martin: That's great!

Jane: I have a game today.

Martin: So do I.

Jane: I play at 2:00 o'clock.

Martin: My game is at 3:00 o'clock.

Jane: It's great fun!

EXERCISES 3 AND 4 – WORKBOOK PAGE 32

LESSON 16   REVIEW

VOCABULARY: wear (to)   The students are to pretend that they have on one or more pictures.

ACTIVITY 1:   **ASK YOUR PARTNER**   **ANSWER IN ORAL SENTENCES**

Do you have <u>a</u> _____? (singular)   Yes, I have <u>a</u> _____.
                                                        No, I don't hav<u>e</u> a _____.
Do you have <u>some</u> _____? (plural)   Yes, I have <u>some</u> _____.
                                                        No, I don't have <u>any</u> _____.

desk

watches

wallet

flower

boats

brush

pants

dress

bicycles

glasses

ring

birds

EXERCISE 1 – WORKBOOK PAGE 33
ORAL QUESTIONS   TEACHER'S GUIDE
ACTIVITY 2 - WORKBOOK PAGE 33
EXERCISES 2 AND 3 – WORKBOOK PAGE 34
ACTIVITY 3 – GUIDE PAGE 67   **TEST 4 – GUIDE PAGES 67-68**

LESSON 17

VOCABULARY:

classroom	in front of	o'clock	curtain
lamp	tree	table	under
beside	behind	iron	stand (to)
teacup	work		

PREPOSITIONS:

ON,   IN,   IN FRONT OF,   AT,   BETWEEN,   BESIDE   UNDER,   BEHIND

This is a table.

A book is on the table.

There is a table <u>in</u> the room.

The table is <u>in front of</u> the window.

There are curtains <u>at</u> the window.

Julia is <u>**at**</u> the table <u>**at**</u> ten o'clock.

She is <u>**between**</u> the table and the window.

There is a lamp <u>**beside**</u> the table.

There is a window <u>**behind**</u> Julia.

Toto is <u>**under**</u> the table.

LESSON 17 CONTINUED

EXERCISE 1 – WORKBOOK PAGE 35

EXERCISE 2 – WORKBOOK PAGE 35

ORAL QUESTIONSTEACHER'S GUIDE

EXERCISE 3 – WORKBOOK PAGE 36

EXERCISE 4 – WORKBOOK PAGE 36

Reference Information

PREPOSITIONS SHOW THE RELATIONSHIP BETWEEN TWO THINGS.

ON - indicates that something is placed on top of something else.
A book is **on** the table.

IN - indicates that something is inside something else.
The table is **in** the room.

AT - indicates a <u>specific</u> place.   The curtains are **at** the window.
or a <u>specific</u> time.   I live **at** 1030 Hulford Street.
We meet **at** eight o'clock.

BETWEEN -indicates that there is something on each side of an object.
Julia is **between** the table and the window.

OF -is often used in a phrase to show a relationship between things.
The table is **in front of** the window.
The book is **on top of** the table.

BESIDE- indicates that something is next to something else.
The lamp is **beside** the table.

UNDER - indicates that an object has something on top of it.
Toto is **under** the table.

BEHIND - indicates that something is at the back of a person or thing.
The window is **behind** Julia.

WITH - indicates that something accompanies a person, place or thing.
Toto is **with** Julia.

LESSON 17 CONTINUED

ACTIVITY 1:   **Discuss the questions with your teacher. Divide into groups.**
Ask these questions. Answer in sentences.

Prepositions and phrases to help you:

between	behind	in front of	under
on the road	at the table	on the table	in her hand

1. Where do they sit?

2. Where is the teacup?

3. Where is the window?

4. Where is their work?

5. Where is the iron?

6. Where is her lunch?

7. Where does she sit?

8. Where are the people?

9. Where is the table?

10. Where is the door?

11. Do they have some books?

12. Where are their feet?

13. Do they read?

LESSON 18

VOCABULARY:	neighbor	many	
now	with	floor	building
address	also	ordinal	someone
third	but	apartment	

ACTIVITY 1:
Listen to your teacher read the paragraphs. Then read the sentences orally for your teacher.

Raymond Carter is Australian. He lives with his family at 11 Kent Street. Raymond's neighbor is Ming. Ming's mother and father are from China, but they are Australian now. He lives at 13 Kent Street. Raymond and Ming are friends. They have a friend Nancy. Nancy is also a friend of Raymond's sister, Ruth. Nancy lives at 15 Kent Street. She lives in an apartment on the third floor.

   Ming, Nancy, Raymond, and Ruth are neighbors. They live on Kent Street.

EXERCISE 1 – WORKBOOK PAGE 37
EXERCISE 2 AND ACTIVITY 2 – WORKBOOK PAGE 38

THE ORDINAL NUMBERS:

first - 1st	second - 2nd	third - 3rd
fourth - 4th	fifth - 5th	sixth - 6th
seventh - 7th	eighth - 8th	ninth - 9th
tenth - 10th	eleventh - 11th	twelfth - 12th
thirteenth - 13th	fourteenth - 14th	fifteenth - 15th
sixteenth - 16th	seventeenth - 17	eighteenth 18th
nineteenth - 19th	twentieth - 20th	twenty-first - 21st
thirtieth - 30th	fortieth - 40th	fiftieth - 50th
sixtieth - 60th	seventieth - 70th	eightieth - 80th
ninetieth - 90th	one hundredth - 100th	one hundred and first

ORAL QUESTIONS   TEACHER'S GUIDE

ACTIVITY 3 – WORKBOOK PAGE 39   **HOW TO PLAY BINGO- GUIDE PAGE 73**
ACTIVITIES 4 AND 5 – GUIDE PAGES 72 AND 73

LESSON 19

VOCABULARY:	foot	paper	put (to)	pocket
	nobody	stone	hand	

Possessive pronouns are <u>not</u> followed by a noun.

SINGULAR	PLURAL This
EXAMPLES: This bicycle is *mine*.	house is *ours*. This
Is this book *yours*?	wallet is *yours*. The
The shoes are *hers*.	desk is *theirs*.
The football is *his*.	

EXERCISE 1 – WORKBOOK PAGE 40

ACTIVITY 1:   **ASK YOUR PARTNER:**

1. Where are your pens?
2. What is beside your chair?
3. What is between you and the window?
4. Who is in front of you?
5. What is on your desk?

6. What is under your book?
7. What is in your desk?
8. Who is at the door?
9. What is beside you?
10. What is behind you?

EXERCISES 2, 3 AND 4 – WORKBOOK PAGES 40 AND 41

ACTIVITY 2:   **FIND A PARTNER:**

To the teacher: Give each pair of students a small object such as a stone. Have the students take turns giving each other the directions as outlined in the chart below. A stone is used as the "object".

Put the stone on a chair.	Put the stone between two pens.
Put the stone behind you.	Put the stone between two books.
Sit on the stone.	Put the stone under a book.
Put the stone between a book and a paper.	Put the stone on your foot.
Put the stone under a picture.	Put the stone in your pocket.
Put the stone between your shoes.	Put the stone beside the window.
Put the stone on the desk.	Put the stone beside your foot.
Put the stone under your foot.	Put the stone in your shoe.

BEGINNERS ESL LESSONS
BOOK 1

STUDENT WORKBOOK

Learning English
Curriculum

Since 1999

www.efl-esl.com

LESSON 1 - Student Workbook

EXERCISE 1:   **Answer in sentences.**

1. What is your name?   _____

2. Who are you?   _____

3. Are you a student?   _____

ACTIVITY 2:

Who is he?   Who are they?

He is Craig.   They are Craig and Jessica.

Who am I?   Who am I?

You are _____.   You are _____.

Who are we?

You _____ Jessica and _____.

Jessica Craig

Who are we?

You _____ Ruth and _____.

Ruth   Raymond

Student Workbook

LESSON 2

EXERCISE 1:   **EXAMPLE:**   **What is your name?**   **My name is** _____ .

1. What is his name? (Craig) _____

2. What is her name? (Jessica) _____

3. What are their names? (Ruth and Raymond) _____

4. What is its name? (dog - Toto) _____

ACTIVITY 4:   **Find a partner:**   **Ask each other:**   **NOTE: The 's means belonging to someone.**

What is your friend's name?   His / Her
_____

What is your teacher's name?   His / Her What
_____

is your mother's name?   Her   What is
_____

your father's name?   His
_____

EXERCISE 2:

1. Does Nancy have a car? _____

2. Is her name Nancy? _____

3. Does Raymond have a motorcycle? _____

4. Does Nancy like motorcycles? _____

5. Do you like motorcycles? _____

EXERCISE 3:
1. Do you have a mother? (yes) _____
2. Do you have a motorcycle? (yes) _____

3. Do you have a car? (yes) _____

4. Do you drive a motorcycle? (yes) _____

5. What is your name? _____

6. Do you like cars? (yes) _____

LESSON 2 CONTINUED

ACTIVITY 6:

Role-play the dialogue together.
Boys are Raymond
Girls are Nancy

TEACHER: Raymond and Nancy are on his motorcycle.

RAYMOND: I like to drive my motorcycle.

NANCY: I like motorcycles and dogs. Do you have a dog?

RAYMOND: Yes, I have a dog.

NANCY: Where is your dog?

RAYMOND: It is outside.

NANCY: Is it friendly?

RAYMOND: Yes, it is a friendly dog.

EXERCISE 4:

Answer in sentences

1. What does Raymond like to do? _____

2. What does Nancy like? _____

3. Who has a dog? _____

4. Where is Raymond's dog? _____

5. Is his dog friendly? _____

6. Do you like friendly dogs? (yes) _____

7. Do you like to drive a motorcycle? (yes) _____

Student Workbook

LESSON 3

Answer these questions in sentences.

EXERCISE 1:

1. Are you hot? _____

2. Are you cold? _____

3. Are you in a restaurant? _____

4. Are you a waiter? _____

5. Are you in an English class? _____

6. Are you a teacher? _____

7. Are you outside? _____

8. Are you thirsty? _____

EXERCISE 2:   **Answer in sentences.**

1. Do they have a dog??

_____

_____

4. Are they in a restaurant??

_____

_____

_____

2. Are they friends??

_____

_____

___

55. Is it a hamburger??

_____

_____

___

3. Do they like pizza??

_____

_____

6. Are they Canadian??

_____

_____

LESSON 3 CONTINUED

ACTIVITY 4:

Role-play the dialogue in unison.
Boys are Peter - Girls are Nancy

Next change roles.

NEW VERB

TO WALK
<u>Singular</u>

Peter:	Do you like to walk, Nancy?
Nancy:	Yes, I like to walk.
Peter:	I like to walk, too.
Nancy:	I like to walk to class.
Peter:	Do you have a car, Nancy?
Nancy:	Yes. I have a car.
Peter:	I do not like to drive cars. I have a motorcycle.
Nancy:	I like to drive motorcycles and cars.

I walk

you walk

he walks

she walks

it walks

<u>Plural</u>

we walk

you walk

they walk

EXERCISE 3: **Answer the questions in sentences.**

1.   Does Nancy like to walk?_____

2.   Does Peter like to walk?_____

3.   Does Nancy like to walk to class?_____

4.   Does Nancy have a car?_____

5.   Does Peter have a motorcycle?_____

6.   Does Peter like to drive cars?_____

7.   Do you like to drive cars?_____

8.   What does Nancy like to drive?_____

LESSON 4

EXERCISE 1:   Use contractions to answer in sentences.

EXAMPLE: **Are they hot? Yes, they're hot.**

1. Are they in an English class? (yes)   _____

2. Is he in a restaurant? (yes)   _____

3. Are you in England?   _____

4. Are you thirsty?   _____

5. Is it cold today?   _____

6. Are we waiters? (yes)   _____

7. Is this your dog?   _____

8. Are they your friends? (yes)   _____

to do –   I don't   we don't
            you don't   you don't
            he doesn't   they don't
            she doesn't
            it doesn't

EXERCISE 2:   Answer in sentences using a contraction of "to do"
EXAMPLE: **Do you have a glass of juice? (no)   No, I don't have a glass of juice.**

1. Do you have a car? (no)   _____

2. Does your friend drink Sprite? (no)   _____

3. Do you want a drink? (no)   _____

4. Do you like motorcycles? (no)   _____

5. Do you have a dog? (no)   _____

6. Do you like pizza? (no)   _____

7. Does your friend drive a car? (no)   _____

8. Do you have a glass of Sprite? (no)   _____

9. Does your friend have a motorcycle? (no)   _____

Student Workbook

LESSON 5

EXERCISE 1:   **Write the answers in sentences.**

1. Where are the friends?   _____

2. What do they do?   _____

3. Does Carol like pasta?   _____

4. Does Tom like pasta?   _____

5. Does Carol like apple juice?   _____

6. Does Sarah like chicken?   _____

7. Does Sarah like hamburgers?   _____

8. Does Peter like pizza?   _____

EXERCISE 2:   **What do they order?**
EXAMPLE: **What <u>does</u> Tom order?   He order<u>s</u> a hamburger.**

1. What does Sarah order?   _____

2. What does Carol order?   _____

3. What does Peter order?   _____

4. Do you eat in a restaurant?   _____

5. What do you order?   _____

6. What does your friend order?   _____

7. Do you make pasta?   _____

8. Do you make hamburgers?   _____

9. Do you drink apple juice?   _____

Student Workbook

LESSON 5 CONTINUED

EXERCISE 3:

Read Page 7 Activity 1 of your Student Book to complete the sentences.
Use these words.

restaurant   mango   all   correct   juice

pizza mistakes   Peter   hamburgers   pasta

Carol, Tom, _____ and Sarah are in the _____ .

Carol orders _____ . Tom doesn't like _____ . He orders _____ .

Peter orders _____ . They _____ want something to drink. They order

_____ .

The waiter makes _____ . The four friends _____ his mistakes.

EXERCISE 4.

MATCH THE MEANING

hamburgers   _____

restaurant   _____

juice   _____

a friend   _____

a glass   _____

cold   _____

thirsty   _____

to drive   _____

you drink it   not hot

you put something to drink in it   you eat them

to make a car go   you like him or her

you eat there   you want something to drink

Student Workbook

LESSON 6

EXERCISE 1:

Complete with the correct form of the verb - <u>to be</u>

1. I _____ a student.

2. They_____students.

3. We _____ inside.

4. He_____ a teacher.

5. She _____ my friend

6. You _____ a student.

EXERCISE 2   **Answer the questions using negative contractions for "to be".**

1. Are you in town? (no) _____

2. Are we in a restaurant? (no) _____

3. Are they Chinese? (no) _____

4. Are you American? (no) _____

5.Is your friend a teacher? (no) _____

6. Are they dogs? (no) _____

EXERCISE 3:   **MATCH THE MEANING**

surname   _____

first   _____

chicken   _____

plural   _____

classmates   _____

mango juice _____

waitress   _____

glass   _____

you eat it   last name   number 1

you drink it   more than one   students in your class

you have something to drink in it   she is in a restaurant

Student Workbook

9

LESSON 6 CONTINUED

EXERCISE 4:

Emily's name is Emily Jane Prescott.
Her first name is Emily.
Her middle name is Jane and her last name (surname) is Prescott.
Her full name is Emily Jane Prescott.

Answer in sentences:

1. What is Emily's full name? _____

2. What is her first name? _____

_____

3. What is her middle name? _____

4. What is her last name? _____

5. What is your first name _____

6. What is your surname? _____

7. What is your full name? _____

_____

EXERCISE 5:

David is a student. He studies English.
His friend Susan is a student.
She studies English too.

Answer in sentences:

1. Is David a student? _____

2. Is Susan David 's friend? _____

3. Is Susan a student? _____

4. Are you a student? _____

5. Do you study English? _____

6. Do you study Spanish, too? _____

Student Workbook

LESSON 7

EXERCISE 1:   Change the sentences to the negative using a contraction.

EXAMPLE: I am a student.   **NEGATIVE:**   I'm not a student.

1. They are students.   **NEGATIVE:** _____

2. We are in the town.   **NEGATIVE:** _____

3. He is a teacher.   **NEGATIVE:** _____

4. They are friends.   **NEGATIVE:** _____

5. It is a dog.   **NEGATIVE:** _____

EXERCISE 2:   **Answer the questions in sentences.**

1. Does the Carter family have a daughter?_____

2. Does the Carter family have a son?_____

3. Does the Carter family have a mother?_____

4. Does the Carter family have a father?_____

5. Do they have a dog?_____

6. Do you have a dog?_____

EXERCISE 3:   Answer in sentences.

1. Are Raymond and George friends?   _____

2. How is Jennifer?   _____

3. What is Jennifer learning?   _____

4. Does Jennifer have brothers?   _____

5. Does she have a sister?   _____

6. Who says "Have a good day"?   _____

7. Do you have brothers and sisters?   _____

Student Workbook

11

LESSON 7 CONTINUED

EXERCISE 4:   **Look at the pictures in the boxes on Page 14.**
Answer these questions in sentences.

EXAMPLE: What is in box number seven? A hat is in box number seven.

1. What is in box number two?   _____

2. What is in box number eleven?   _____

3. What is in box number six?   _____

4. What is in box number one?   _____

5. What is in box number three?   _____

6. What is in box number twelve?   _____

7. What is in box number five?   _____

8. What is in box number ten?   _____

9. What is in box number nine?   _____

10. What is in box number four?   _____

11. What is in box number seven?   _____

12. What is in box number eight?   _____

EXERCISE 5:   **MATCH THE MEANING**

family   _____

son   _____

daughter   _____

fine   _____

How do you do? _____

Nice to meet you. _____

tea   _____

mine   _____

cup   _____

informal introduction	a mother and father's boy	good
a hot drink	it's yours	mother, father, son, daughter
formal introduction	a mother and father's girl	you drink from it

Student Workbook

LESSON 7 CONTINUED

to go

Singular	**Plural**
I go	we go
you go	you go
he goes	they go
she goes	
it goes	

EXERCISE 6:   **Write the correct words on the lines.**

Use these words:

church	Canada	motorcycles	school
walk	drive	English	Canadian

David is from Canada. He is _____. He has a friend.

Her name is Mary. She is Canadian. She's from _____. David has a motorcycle.

He likes _____.

Mary has a car. She doesn't drive a motorcycle. She likes to _____ her car to

the city. Sometimes she goes to the _____.

David drives his motorcycle to _____. He studies _____. Mary likes

Canada. She wants to study _____ history.

EXERCISE 7:   **Answer the questions in sentences.**

1. Is Mary a boy or a girl?   _____

2. Where is David from?   _____

3. Where is Mary from?   _____

4. Does Mary have a motorcycle?   _____

5. What does Mary want to study?   _____

Student Workbook

LESSON 8

EXERCISE 1:

Answer the questions in sentences.

1. What is this?

_____

2. Is this a bird?

_____

3. Do you have a tie?

_____

4. What is this?

_____

55. Do you have a cat?

_____

66. What is this?

_____

77. Is this a jacket?

_____

8. Is this a shoe?

_____

99. Does a house have a door?

_____

10. Are they friends?

_____

11. Does she have a daughter?

_____

12. Do Nancy and
    Raymond meet?

_____

13. Does he have a son?

_____

14. What is this?

_____

LESSON 8 CONTINUED

Craig and Jessica are the father and mother.

Raymond Carter is their son.

Ruth Carter is their daughter.

Their dog is Toto.

EXERCISE 2:   **Answer in sentences**

1. What is the Carter's dog's name?_____

2. Does Craig have a son and a daughter? _____

3. Does Jessica have a daughter?_____

4. What is Craig's son's name? _____

5. Who is Raymond's mother? _____

6. Who is Jessica's daughter? _____

7. Do you have a dog?_____

8. Do you have a son?_____

9. Do you have a daughter?_____

10. Do you have a sister? _____

11. Do you have a brother? _____

12. Do you live in town? _____

Student Workbook

LESSON 9

EXERCISE 1:
EXAMPLES:

ANSWERS	YOU WRITE THE QUESTIONS.
He has a cup of coffee.	Does he have a cup of coffee?
It is a good restaurant.	Is it a good restaurant?

1. She has a hamburger. _____?

2. They are in English class. _____?

3. He meets a friend. _____?

4. They walk to town. _____?

5. His last name is Carter. _____?

6. Yes, the Carters have a dog. _____?

7. No, I don't like coffee. _____?

EXERCISE 2: **Answer using to be or to do.**
The verb to do isn't used with the verb to be.

EXAMPLES:

Do you have a daughter?	No, I don't have a daughter.
Are you in English class?	Yes, I'm in English class.

1. Is your name Dale? _____

2. Do you have a cat? _____

3. Is the Carter family French? (no) _____

4. Does Ruth Carter have a bird? _____

5. Do you have a dog? _____

6. Are you a student? _____

7. Are they in town? (yes) _____

8. Does Craig Carter have a son? _____

9. Are you learning English? _____

Student Workbook

16

LESSON 9 CONTINUED

POSSESSIVES:
Possessives also use an apostrophe (') to express possession.
EXAMPLES: grandfather's name   Mark's father   his sister's book

EXERCISE 3:   **Answer these questions in sentences.**

EXAMPLE: My friend's name is _____.   I don't have a friend.

1. What is your friend's name?

_____

2. What is your mother's first name?

_____

3. What is your father's last name?

_____

4. What is your brother's name?

_____

5. What is your sister's name?

_____

6. What is your grandmother's name?

_____

7. What is your grandfather's name?

EXERCISE 4:   **Use these words to complete the sentences.**

1. Is this your father's book?   pleased   house   glass   thirsty

                               tea   shake   hot   Mrs.

Susan and John go to John's grandparents'_____. Susan meets his grandparents, Mr. _____

and _____ Johnson. They are _____ to meet her. They all _____hands.

Grandfather is_____. He needs a cup of _____. Mrs. Johnson, John's grandmother, says

she is _____. She wants to have a _____ of cold mango juice.

Student Workbook

LESSON 9 CONTINUED

ACTIVITY 3:   **Ask a partner**
Answer in sentences Use reported speech

EXAMPLE: Do you have a daughter?
Yes, he / she has a daughter.   No, he / she doesn't have a daughter.
OR   Yes, (student's name) has a daughter.   No, (student's name) doesn't have a daughter.

1. Do you have a window in your house? _____

2. Do you have two shoes? _____

3. Do you have a husband? _____

4. Do you have a bird in your house? _____

5. Do you have a wife? _____

6. Do you have a sister? _____

7. Do you have a door in your house? _____

8. Do you have a brother? _____

9. Is your friend in town? _____

10. **EXERCISE 5:**   **Answer the questions in sentences.**

1. Does Susan meet John's grandparents for the first time? _____

2. Does John's grandfather like tea? _____

3. Are the grandparents pleased to meet Susan? _____

4. What does Susan have to drink? _____

5. What do you like to drink? _____

Student Workbook

LESSON 10

ACTIVITY 2:   **Ask your partner.**   **Use reported speech.**   **EXAMPLES:**

Where are you from??   He's / She's from FFrance.   No, he's she's not from France.

Are you American??   Yes, he's / she's American.   No, he's she's not American.

1. Where are you from?   He's /She's _____

2. Are you English?   _____, he's / she's _____

3. Are you from Russia?   He's / She's_____

4. Where is your mother from?   She's_____

5. Where is your father from?   He's _____

ACTIVITY 3:   **FIND A PARTNER**   **USE REPORTED SPEECH:**

Ask your partner these questions.

Raise your hand to indicate "he" or "she" or "they

EXAMPLE: Does he have a hat??

Yes, he has a hat.

1. Does she have a cat?   _____

2. Does he have a dog?   _____

3. Does he have a car?   _____

4. Does she have a Sprite?   _____

5. Do they have a pen?   _____

6. Does he have a jacket?   _____

7. Does she have a notebook?   _____

8. Does she have a book?   _____

9. Do they have juice?   _____

10. Does she have a bird?   _____

Student Workbook

LESSON 10 CONTINUED

EXERCISE 1:   **THE CARTER FAMILY**   **ANSWER IN SENTENCES.**

1. Do the Carters have a cat?   _____

2. Does Ruth have a son? (no)   _____

3. Does Craig Carter have a daughter?   _____

4. Does Raymond have a grandfather? (no)   _____

5. Does Jessica have a grandmother? (no)   _____

6. Does Craig have a sister? (no)   _____

7. Does Raymond have a brother? (no)   _____

8. Does Ruth have a friend? (yes)   _____

9. Does the Carter family have a dog?   _____

10. Does Jessica have an English teacher?(no) _____

EXERCISE 2:
    Answer these questions using contractions (Page 6 / 10) and / or possessive adjectives (Page 2).

EXAMPLES :   They live in China.   What is their nationality??   They're Chinese.

     Kate has a brother Bill.   Who is Bill??   He's Kate's brother.

1. She is from Tibet.   What is her nationality? _____

2. Rita has a jacket.   Whose jacket is it? _____

3. Nancy and Mark are outside.   Where are they? _____

44. We are from Canada.   What is our nationality? _____

55. Bill and Maria are in class.   Where are they? _____

6. John has a dog.   Whose dog is it? _____

7. Margaret has a son.   Whose son is he? _____

8. Mary has a book.   Whose book is it? _____

9. David is Canadian.   Where is he from? _____

Student Workbook

LESSON 11

EXERCISE 1:   **Answer these questions in sentences:**

1. Who does Harry meet?   _____

2. Are they friends?   _____

3. How is Jane?   _____

4. How is Harry?   _____

5. How are you?   _____

6. How are you doing?   _____

EXERCISE 2:   **Answer these questions in sentences:**

1. Is Harry Jane's friend?   _____

2. Is Jane sick?   _____

3. How is Harry?   _____

4. What does Jane ask Harry?   _____

5. How are you doing?   _____

6. Are you sick?   _____

EXERCISE 3:   **Here are the answers. Write the questions:**

1. I am fine, thank you.   _____?

2. Things are going well at school. _____?

3. I'm doing very well, thanks.   _____?

4. I'm not so good.   _____?

5. I'm okay.   _____?

I'm okay, too!

I'm not so good.

Student Workbook

LESSON 11 CONTINUED

EXERCISE 4:   **MATCH THE MEANING**

Write the meaning beside each word.

sick   _____

bad   _____

at home   _____

well   _____

week   _____

notebook   _____

grandparents   _____

coffee   _____

pen   _____ _

How do you do? _____

negative   _____

door   _____

formal introduction	you write <u>in</u> it	not good
your mother or father's mother and father	you drink it	fine
where you walk into a room	you write <u>with</u> it	seven days
where you live	not well	no

EXERCISE 5:   **Use these words to complete the sentences.**

juice	**today**	**sick**	**gives**	**notebook**	**how**
not so good	**wants**	**Hi**	**town**	**says**	

Harry is_____ at home from school _____ . He _____ to have some mango

_____ . He goes to _____ where he meets Jane.

She says, _____ Harry, _____ _are you?" He says he's _____ _.

Jane _____ Harry her English _____ . He _____ ,

"Thanks Jane."

Student Workbook

LESSON 12

EXERCISE 1:   **Answer the questions in sentences:**

1. Are they meeting?   _____

2. Are they shaking hands?   _____

3. Do you usually shake hands?   _____

4. What do they say when they shake hands? _____

5. Is it a formal introduction?   _____

6. Do they have hats?   _____

7. Is Toto a cat?   _____

8. Is Carter their last name?   _____

9. What is the dog's name?   _____

10. Does Raymond have a father? _____

11. Does Craig have a wife?   _____

12. Does Ruth have a husband?   _____

13. Are they a family?   _____

14. Is Toto their dog?   _____

15. Do they have shoes?   _____

16. Is Ruth French? (no)   _____

17. What is in his hand?   _____

18. Does he have a jacket? _____

Student Workbook

23

LESSON 12 CONTINUED

EXERCISE 2:   **REVIEW**

1. Are they friends?

2. Does the house have a door?

3. Are they brothers?

_____

_____

_____

4. Are they from Paris?

5. Is he a mother?

6. Are they sisters?

_____

_____

_____

7. Is this your hat?

8. Is this your friend's cup?

9. Are they dogs?

_____

_____

_____

10. Is she your daughter?

11. Do you have a book?

12. Is this your sister's jacket?

_____

_____

_____

LESSON 12 CONTINUED

EXERCISE 3:

Answer the following questions in sentences.

1. Where is your dog? _____

2. What is your surname? _____

3. What is your mother's name? _____

4. What city do you live in? _____

5. What country do you live in? _____

6. Do the Carters have a dog? _____

7. What is their dog's name? _____

8. Is Raymond Carter a boy? _____

9. What are they? _____

10. Does Ruth have a brother? _____

_11. What is Ruth's brother's name?_____

_____

12. Is Ruth Jessica's son? _____

13. Does Jessica have a daughter? _____

_____

14. What is your friend's name? _____

_____

15. What country are you from? _____

16. Do you have a brother? _____

17. Are your friends American? _____

18. Does your mother live in Portugal?_____

19. Do you have a sister? _____

20. What city do you live in? _____

Student Workbook

LESSON 13

EXERCISE 1:　　　　　　　**Write the plural of the following nouns:**

bridge _____　　　watch _____　　　face _____　　　ring _____

girl _____　　　church _____　　　wallet _____　　　page _____

dictionary _____　　　book _____　　　glass _____　　　toy _____

desk _____　　　pencil _____　　　box _____　　　match _____

dish _____　　　dress _____　　　boy _____　　　pen _____

EXERCISE 2:　　　**Find a partner. Answer using reported speech.**　　　**(Do <u>not</u> use the negative)**

EXAMPLE:　　　　　How many pencils do you have?　　　He / She has one pencil.

1. How many books do you have?　　　_____

2. How many watches do you have?　　_____

3. How many faces do you have?　　　_____

4. How many pens do you have?　　　_____

5. How many notebooks do you have?_____

6. How many friends do you have?　　_____

EXERCISE 3: _____　　　　　**Name these objects:**

_____　　　_____　　　_____　　　_____

_____　　　_____　　　_____　　　_____

LESSON 13 CONTINUED

EXERCISE 4:

Use these words to complete the dialogue below.

so many	books	Canada	desks	class
window	write	nice	home	mistakes

NARRATOR: Carol and Tom are talking about their English _____ in_____. This is a

CAROL: very _____room.

TOM: We have _____ good things. We have comfortable _____, interesting

_____ and a good board for our teacher to _____on. I like all the

CAROL: students. We laugh and talk about our _____.

I like to look out the _____ at the mountains.

TOM: I like English classes. I study at _____.

CAROL: So do I!

EXERCISE 5:   **MATCH THE MEANING**

classroom   _____

shake hands   _____

comfortable   _____

interesting   _____

notebook   _____

partner   _____

numbers   _____

desks   _____

home   _____

you write in it	nice to sit on	a school room
a friend you work with	one, two, three…	you do it when you are introduced
you sit at them to write	where you live	you want to know more

LESSON 14

EXERCISE 1:   **ANSWER IN SENTENCES**
EXAMPLE: **Do you have a bird?   Yes, I have a bird.   No, I don't have a bird.**

1. Do you have a wallet?   _____

2. Do you have a desk?   _____

3. Does your mother have a ring?   _____

4. Do you have a face?   _____

5. Do you have a necklace?   _____

6. Do you have a father in Canada?   _____

7. Do you have an American sister?_____

EXERCISE 2:

                Here are the answers.   You write the questions.
EXAMPLE: **I don't have any hamburgers.   Do you have some hamburgers?**

1. She doesn't have any coffee.   _____

2. I don't have any juice.   _____

3. They have some cars.   _____

ACTIVITY 1:   **ASK YOUR PARTNER.**
                    Use reported speech.

1. Do you have some dogs?   _____

2. Does (name) have some necklaces?   _____

3. Do you have some rings?   _____

4. Do you have some matches?   _____

5. Are there some pages in your book?   _____

6. Does your friend have some cats?   _____

LESSON 14 CONTINUED

ACTIVITY 2:   **Divide the students into groups of two.**
From the Student Reader, Page 25, photocopy one set of pictures for each group.

For a group of three, give two students the <u>Student 1</u> questions
and the third the <u>Student 2</u> questions.

Give each group one set of picture cards and have them deal them out.
The students are to ask each other the questions on their question sheet
and write the answers using reported speech.

They begin each sentence with He / She

EXAMPLE: **Yes, he <u>has</u> a watch.**   **No, he <u>doesn't have</u> a watch**

STUDENT 1

Do you have a watch?   _____

Do you have a wallet?   _____

Do you have a ring?   _____

Do you have a pencil?   _____

Do you have a face?   _____

Do you have a dress?   _____

Do you have a box?   _____

Do you have a desk?   _____

Do you have a glass?   _____

Do you have a toy?   _____

Do you have a match?   _____

Do you have a face?   _____

Do you have a page?   _____

Do you have a ring?   _____

Do you have a dish?   _____

Do you have a pen?   _____

Do you have a pencil?   _____

LESSON 14 CONTINUED

EXERCISE 3:

Use "some" in question and positive sentences.
Use "any" in a negative plural sentence.

EXAMPLES:

Does she have some boxes??
Yes, she has some boxes.

Do they have some boxes? No,
they don't have any boxes.

Look at the pictures and answer these questions in sentences.

1. Do you see some mountains?

_____

2. Do you see some motorcycles?

_____

3. Do they have some chairs?

_____

4. Do you see some bridges?

_____

5. Do the students have some desks?

_____

LESSON 15

EXERCISE 1:   Answer in sentences using object pronouns.

EXAMPLE: Do you have my_pen?   Yes, I have it.   No, I don't have it.

1. Do you see Marie?   _____

2. Do you see my dog?   _____

3. Do you see Robert?   _____

4. Do you see your family?   _____

5. Do you have my book?   _____

6. Do you have my glasses?   _____

7. Do you have my dress?   _____

8. Do you have my cat?   _____

9. Do you see Marie and Robert?   _____
_____
10. Do you see John?   _____

EXERCISE 2:   Complete the sentences with a, an, or the.

1. They have _____ cat.

2. _____ man's name is John.

3. There is _____ church.

4. _____ dog, Toto, is here.

5. He sees _____ car.

6. There is _____ apple.

7. _____ first lesson is here.

8. There is _____ toy.

9. She has _____ desk.

10. They go to _____ small theater.

John

Student Workbook

LESSON 15 CONTINUED

Complete the following sentences using <u>a</u>, <u>an</u> or <u>the</u>.

EXERCISE 3:

1. Do you have _____ friend? Yes, I have _____ friend.

2. Who is _____ teacher? _ _____ teacher is _____.

3. Can I have _____ pen?   Here is _____ apple.
4. Where is _____ apple?
5. Does she have _____ son?   No, she doesn't have _____ son.

6. Do some people have _____ middle name? Yes, they have _____ middle name.

7. Where is _____ red English book?   _____ red English book is here. Yes,

8. Do you go to _____ big theater?   I go to _____ big theater.

9. Do you see _____ cat? No, I don't see _____ cat.

10. What is _____ verb in this sentence? _____ verb is _____ "in the sentence.

EXERCISE 4:
Answer the questions in sentences using an object pronoun instead of the underlined words.

1. Do you have <u>my book</u>? _____

2. Do you meet <u>your friends</u>? _____

3. Do you do <u>your work</u>? _____

4. Do you see <u>your grandfather</u>? _____

5. Do you see <u>your family</u>? _____

6. Do you like <u>Marie</u>? _____

7. Do you see the <u>cats</u>? _____

8. Do you see a <u>bird</u>? _____

Student Workbook

https://www.efl-esl.com

LESSON 16

EXERCISE 1:   **Write the plural:**

1. watch   _____

2. brush   _____

3. dress   _____

4. glasses   _____

5. face   _____

6. church   _____

7. pen   _____

8. ring   _____

9. wallet   _____

10. necklace   _____

USE REPORTED SPEECH

ACTIVITY 2:   **ASK YOUR PARTNER**

EXAMPLES: How many desks are in this class?   There are 12 desks.
Does ____ have a T-shirt?   (name) ____ has a T-shirt.   (name) _____ doesn't have a T-shirt.

1. How many students are in this class? _____

2. How many pens do you have? _____

3. Do you wear glasses? _____

4. How many birds are there in Activity 1? _____
    (see page 31 Student Reader)

5. How many boys are in this class? _____

6. How many pencils are on this desk? _____

7. How many pages are in your book? _____

8. How many churches are in this city? _____

9. Does your dog speak English? _____

10. Does your cat read books? _____

11. Does your book have twenty pages? _____

Student Workbook

LESSON 16 CONTINUED

EXERCISE 2:   **Answer the questions using an object pronoun.**

EXAMPLE: **Do you have the <u>red jacket</u>?**   **Yes, I have <u>it</u>.**

1. Do you see your <u>friends</u>?   _____

2. Do you have your <u>wallet</u>?   _____

3. Do you read <u>books</u>?   _____

4. Do you see the <u>girl</u>? (no)   _____

5. Does the man have his <u>hat</u>? (no)   _____

6. Can you meet my <u>family</u>? (no)   _____

7. Do you and your friend see some <u>boats</u>? (no)   _____

8. Do you see the <u>man</u>? (no)   _____

EXERCISE 3:   **Use negative contractions for: <u>to be</u>, <u>to have</u> and <u>to do</u>.**

        EXAMPLE: Is her surname Smith? (no)   No, her surname **<u>isn't</u>** Smith.

1. Does he have a tie? (no)   _____

2. Is this London? (no)   _____

3. Are you a mother? (no)   _____

4. Does she have a hat? (no)   _____

5. Does she drink Sprite? (no)   _____

6. Are you a grandfather? (no)   _____

7. Are the students outside? (no)   _____

8. Are they Canadians? (no)   _____

Student Workbook

LESSON 17

EXERCISE 1:   Use these prepositions to complete the sentences.

on   behind   in   under   beside   between   in front of

1. The lady is _____ the elephant.

2. The man is _____ the car.

3. The dog is _____ the lady.

4. The cat is _____ the house.

5. The elephant and the car are _____ the house.

6. The man is _____ the tree.

7. The door is_____ the windows.

8. The tree is _____ the house.

EXERCISE 2:   ANSWER THESE QUESTIONS IN SENTENCES

1. Where is the tree? _____

2. Where is the elephant? _____

3. Where is the dog? _____

4. Where is the door? _____

5. Where is the man? _____

Student Workbook

LESSON 17 CONTINUED

EXERCISE 3:

You are sitting in your classroom.

Answer the following questions in sentences using the correct prepositions.

1. Is your dog in front of <u>you</u>? _____

2. Where is your <u>teacher</u>? _____

3. Where are your <u>books</u>? _____

4. What is under <u>you</u>? _____

5. Is your cat with <u>you</u>? _____

6. Where is your <u>friend</u>? _____

7. What (who) is behind <u>you</u>? _____

8. Where is your <u>pen</u>? _____

9. What is on your <u>desk</u>? _____

10. Are the <u>pictures</u> on the wall? _____

EXERCISE 4:   **OBJECT PRONOUNS**   **REVIEW OF "A" and "THE"**

Complete the sentences.

1. Our cat is _____ big one. Do you see _____?_

2. Here is _____ good book. It is for _____.

3. They are _____ English teachers. Do you like _____ ?

4. We are _____ students. Do you see _____ ?

5. Here is _____ teacher.

6. They are my dogs. Do you like _____ ?

7. The gray dog is friendly. Do you want _____ ?

8. This is _____ toy. You can have _____.

Student Workbook

LESSON 18

Answer in sentences

EXERCISE 1:

1. Is Raymond Carter Australian??

_____

2. What country does Ming live in?

_____

3. Where do Ming's parents come from?

_____

4. What is Raymond Carter's address?

_____

5. Who lives on the third floor of the apartment building?

_____

6. Is Ming Chinese?

_____

7. What is Raymond's sister's name?

_____

8. What is Ming's address?

_____

9. Who is Ruth's friend?

_____

10. Who are Raymond and Ruth's neighbors?

_____

11. What street do Raymond and Ruth live on?

_____

12. What street do you live on?

LESSON 18 CONTINUED

EXERCISE 2:   **MATCH THE MEANING**

neighbor   _____

apartment   _____

classroom   _____

many people have homes in one building   someone who lives beside you
the room where you learn from your teacher

ACTIVITY 2:

Use 'at'"if there is a number.   **Example:** <u>at</u> 11 Kent Street.
Use 'on' if there isn't a number.   **Example:** <u>on</u> Kent Street.
Use "in" for a city or country.

There are many students in this room. Ask two students the following questions.
Answer in sentences.
EXAMPLES: He / She lives <u>at</u> 11 Kent Street .   He / She lives <u>on</u> Kent Street.
He / She lives <u>in</u> Melbourne.

****

FIRST STUDENT:
Where do you live? (street)   _____

Where do you live? (give street and number)

_____

City: _____

What is your address?   _____

_____ Postal Code: _____

****

SECOND STUDENT:
Where do you live? (street)   _____

Where do you live? (give street and number)

_____

City: _____

What   is   your   address??

_____

_____ Postal Code: _____

******<u>Student Workbook</u>**   38

LESSON 18 CONTINUED

ACTIVITY 3:   **BINGO**

(See Guide page 73 of Book 1 Part 1 for instructions about how to play.)

MATCH THE MEANING:
Write the words in LIST 1 into the boxes.
When these words are called put a small x in the corner of the box with the
word that has a similar meaning.

LIST 1	WORDS TO PRINT			
one	two	three	four	five
six	seven	eight	nine	ten
eleven	twelve	thirteen	fourteen	fifteen
sixteen	seventeen	eighteen	nineteen	twenty
twenty	twenty-one	twenty-two	twenty-three	twenty-four

LIST 2	WORDS TO CALL			
first	second	third	fourth	fifth
sixth	seventh	eighth	nineth	tenth
eleventh	twelfth	thirteenth	fourteenth	fifteenth
sixteenth	seventeenth	eighteenth	nineteenth	twentieth
twenty-first	twenty-second	twenty-third	twenty-fourth	

		BINGO		

Student Workbook

LESSON 19

EXERCISE 1:   **Complete the sentences using possessive pronouns.** Is

EXAMPLE: this your dog??   Yes, it's <u>mine</u>.

1. Is this your dog? (yes)

_____

2. Whose classroom is this?

_____

3. This is Jane's necklace. Whose is it?

_____

4. Is this John and Mary's house?

_____

5. Your name is on this book. Whose book is it?

_____

6. Is this our book?

_____

7. Is this Peter's radio?

_____

8. Are they their books?

_____

EXERCISE 2:   **Answer these questions in sentences using: <u>there is / there are</u>:**

1. How many students are here?   _____

2. How many books are on the desk?   _____

3. How many desks are here?   _____

4. How many teachers are here?   _____

5. How many pens are on your desk?   _____

EXERCISE 3:   **Answer these questions in sentences.**

1. Where is your pen?   _____

2. Where is your book?   _____

3. Who is behind you?   _____

4. What is in front of you?   _____

5. What is under your book?   _____

6. Who is beside you?   _____

Student Workbook

LESSON 19 CONTINUED

EXERCISE 4: Complete the following sentences using any of the following prepositions or prepositional phrases.

in,   at,   on,   with,   beside,   in front of,   between,   behind,   under

1.   I live _____ a house.

2.   I get up _____ ten o'clock.

3.   I sit _____my desk.

4.   I live _____ (city name).

5.   I go to school /work _____ my friend.

6.   We live _____ our neighbors.

7.   They are _____ the city.

8.   I sit _____ my friend.

9.   No one is _____ the bridge.

10.   The water is _____ the bridge.

11.   The teacher is _____ me.

12.   The toy is _____ the box.

13.   The door is _____ me.

14.   I study English _____ my friends.

15.   She lives _____ an apartment.

16.   She lives _____ the third floor.

Student Workbook

LESSON 20   REVIEW

Answer the questions in sentences using an object pronoun.

EXERCISE 1:

1. Do you have your <u>books</u>?   _____

2. Do you see the <u>teacher</u>?   _____

3. Does this city have <u>churches</u>?_____

4. Do you see the <u>dog</u>?   _____

5. Do you meet your <u>friends</u>?   _____

6. Do you see your <u>friends</u>?   _____

7. Do you see Mary's <u>house</u>?   _____

8. Do you speak <u>German</u>?   _____

EXERCISE 2:   **Answer the questions in sentences using one of these prepositions.**

on	in	at	in front of	between	beside	under	behind

1. Where is your pen?   _____

2. Who is at the door?   _____

3. Who is beside you?   _____

4. Who is between ____ and ___?   _____

5. What is in front of you??
                                  _____
6. What is under your desk?
                                  _____

EXERCISE 3:   **Answer the questions using these possessive pronouns.**

mine	yours	his	hers	its	ours	yours	theirs

1. This is my book. Whose book is it?   _____

2. The students have pens. Whose pens are they?   _____

3. Whose classroom is this?   _____

4. The boy has a toy. Whose toy is it?   _____

Student Workbook

GLOSSARY

ENGLISH	NOTES	ENGLISH	NOTES
address		desk	
adjective		dialogue	
all		dish	
also		do (to), did	
and		dog	
answer (to), answered		door	
any		dress	
apartment		drink (to), drank	
apple		drive (to), drove	
ask (to), asked		eat (to), ate	
at home		face	
bad		family	
be (to), am, is, are		father	
behind		find (to), found	
beside		fine	
big		first	
bird		floor	
blouse		foot	
box (boxes)		football	
boy		formal	
bridge		four	
bring (to), brought		friend	
brother		from	
brown		full	
building		girl	
but		girls	
buy (to), bought		give (to), gave	
can		glass	
car		glasses	
cat		go (to), went	
chair		good	
Cheers!		good bye	
chicken		grammar	
church		grandfather	
city		grandmother	
class		great	
classmate		hamburger	
classroom		hand	
coffee		handle	
cold		hat	
come (to), came		have (to), had	
comfortable		hello	
correct (to), corrected		her	
country		here's	
cup of tea		Hi	
curtain		his	
daughter		history	

Student Workbook

GLOSSARY CONTINUED

# ENGLISH	NOTES	ENGLISH	NOTES
hot		noun	
house		now	
how about…?		number	
how many		o'clock	
husband		on	
idea		one (pronoun)	
in		ordinal	
in front of		our	
interesting		outside	
iron		page	
its		paper	
jacket		partner	
juice		pasta	
just		pen	
know (to), knew		pencil	
lady		people	
lamp		picture	
language		pizza	
last		please (to), pleased	
learn (to), learned		plural	
like (to), liked		pocket	
list		possessive	
live (to), lived		preposition	
look (to), looked		pronoun	
look for (to), looked for		put (to), put	
man		read (to), read	
mango		red	
many		restaurant	
match		ring	
men		robe	
middle		room	
mistake		say (to), said	
mother		see (to), saw	
motorcycle		sentence	
mountain		shoe	
Mr. / Mrs. / Ms.		sick	
my		singular	
name		sister	
nationality		sit (to), sat	
necklace		sit down (to), sat down	
need (to), needed		six	
negative		some	
neighbor		someone	
new		son	
nice		so-so	
no		speak (to), spoke	
nobody		specific	
not		Sprite	

Student Workbook

GLOSSARY CONTINUED

ENGLISH	NOTES	ENGLISH	NOTES
stone		under	
student		usually	
study (to), studied		verb	
surname		very	
table		waiter	
talk about (to), talked about		waitress	
tea		walk (to), walked	
teacher		wallet	
teacup		want (to), wanted	
thank you		watch	
theater		wear (to), wore	
their		week	
there are		well	
there is		what	
things		where	
third		white	
thirsty		who	
this		whose	
tie		wife	
time		window	
today		with	
too		woman	
town		women	
toy		work	
tree		write (to), wrote	
T-shirt		your	
umbrella		yours	

Student Workbook

BEGINNERS ESL LESSONS BOOK 1

TEACHER'S GUIDE

Learning English
Curriculum
Since 1999
www.efl-esl.com

TEACHER'S GUIDE

An Interactive Structured Approach to Learning English

This Series Includes a Student Reader, Student Workbook and a Teacher's Guide.

This Teacher's Guide provides answers to all Student Reader and Workbook questions. It also includes Oral Questions for every lesson. Throughout our years of teaching in a number of countries, students consistently gave the Oral Question the highest rating on our surveys. This Teacher's Guide also provides conversational activities, competitive games in Large and Small Groups, four unit Tests and a Mid-term Test.

Teachers   Guide   LESSON 1

At the beginning of the first class the teacher will introduce himself or herself by saying,
My name is _____.
We suggest that the students could then introduce themselves by saying,
My name is _____."
As this is our International Edition we have included a variety of English names in this book.
Our experience has shown us that many students have difficulty identifying the male names and
the female names. Lists are provided as a part of the several lessons to help them with this.

INTRODUCING THE NEW VOCABULARY IN EACH LESSON
Each teacher will find their own method for helping the students to understand the new words.
We suggest writing the words on the board as they are explained. Possible ways for making their
meaning clear might include: dramatizing, drawing, pointing to objects or pictures or using the
words in sentences with vocabulary that has been already introduced.

The Oral Questions are the most important activity or exercise.
Without these the content will become too difficult.
This has been verified by surveys given to thousands of students in many countries.
The **oral questions** are based on what is taught in the lesson, and should be asked many times
until the students can answer fluently without stopping to think.
We suggest that each Oral Question session should review the oral questions from the preceding
lesson(s, and then proceed to those for the new lesson. When the students have difficulty with a
question it should be put on the blackboard with the sentence answer.

ORAL QUESTIONS
Tell the students that in English the second person singular and plural of "to be" are the same.
Example: <u>Are you</u> a student? <u>Are you</u> students?

singular	plural
What is your name?	*My name is _____.*
Are you a student?	*Yes, I am a student.*
Is your friend a student?	*Yes, my friend is a student.*

PAGE 1   **ACTIVITY 1:**
We suggest that the students speak in unison to read the answers to these early
question and answer activities.
This method is well suited to groups that are involved with chanting in their own culture. It also
provides a cover for those who are shy about articulating the new sounds of the English
language.
Directions are provided with each activity.

PAGE 1   **ANSWERS TO THE WORKBOOK QUESTIONS**   **EXERCISE 1:**
1.   What is your name?   *My name is _____.*
2.   Who are you?   *I am _____.*
3.   Are you a student?   *Yes, I'm a student.*

LESSON 1 CONTINUED

PAGE 1   **ANSWERS TO THE WORKBOOK QUESTIONS** **ACTIVITY 2:**

Who am I?	*You are Craig.*	Who am I? You are Jessica.
Who are we?	*You are Jessica and Craig.*	
Who are we?	*You are Ruth and Raymond.*	

ACTIVITY 3:   **PAGE 3 OF THIS GUIDE**

Photocopy the questions and answers on Page 3 of this guide and cut them into separate cards.
Divide the students into two teams - TEAM 1 and TEAM 2.
Move the chairs so that the teams are facing each other.
Give out all the questions so that each student has at least one.
Some can have more than one.

A student in TEAM 1 asks a member of TEAM 2 the question on his or her card.
If the answer is correct the team gets one point.
Next a student on TEAM 2 asks a member of TEAM 1 the question on his or her card.
Each student should answer at least one question.

Tell the students to answer "Yes" plus the rest of the sentence to all the questions.

All questions are answered in sentences.

Teacher Guide

LESSON 1 CONTINUED

ACTIVITY 3:

What is your name?
My name is _____.

Is your friend a student?
Yes, my friend is a student.

What is your teacher's name?
My teacher's name is _____.

Are you a student?
Yes, I am a student.

Is your friend in English class?
Yes, my friend is in English class.

Who is your friend?
_____ *is my friend.*

Are dogs friendly?
Yes, dogs are friendly.

Are dogs in restaurants?
Yes, dogs are in restaurants.

Is your teacher your friend?
Yes, my teacher is my friend.

Are you an English student?
Yes, I am an English student.

Who are you?
I am _____.

Who is your English teacher?
_____ *is my English teacher.*

LESSON 2

Note to the teacher:
"dogs" – In some cultures, dogs are very important. For example, in the Czech Republic where many people have a dog, they are an important part of everyday living. Mature adults will tell you that their dog is their best friend. Although this may seem to be ridiculous in one culture it is a fact in another.

ORAL QUESTIONS

Do you like dogs?	*Yes, I like dogs.*
Do you have a motorcycle? (yes)	*Yes, I have a motorcycle.*
Do you like to drive a car? (yes)	*Yes, I like to drive a car.*
Do you have a car? (yes)	*Yes, I have a car.*
Do you like restaurants? (yes)	*Yes, I like restaurants.*
Do you like your friends? (yes)	*Yes, I like my friends.*

PAGE 2　　　**ANSWERS TO THE WORKBOOK QUESTIONS**　　　**EXERCISE 1:**

1. What is his name? (Craig)	*His name is Craig.*
2. What is her name? (Jessica)	*Her name is Jessica.*
3. What are their names? (Ruth and Raymond)	*Their names are Ruth and Raymond.*
4. What is its name? (dog - Toto)	*Its name is Toto.*

PAGE 2　　　**ANSWERS TO THE WORKBOOK QUESTIONS**　　　**ACTIVITY 4:**

What is your *friend's* name?	His / Her *name is* _____.
What is your *teacher's* name?	His / Her *name is* _____.
What is your *mother's* name?	Her *name is* _____.
What is your *father's* name?	His *name is* _____.

PAGE 2　　　**ANSWERS TO THE WORKBOOK QUESTIONS**　　　**EXERCISE 2:**

1. Does Nancy have a car?	*Yes, Nancy has a car.*
2. Is her name Nancy?	*Yes, her name is Nancy.*
3. Does Raymond have a motorcycle?	*Yes, Raymond has a motorcycle.*
4. Does Nancy like motorcycles?	*Yes, Nancy likes motorcycles.*
5. Do you like motorcycles?	*Yes, I like motorcycles.*

LESSON 2 CONTINUED

PAGE 2 **ANSWERS TO THE WORKBOOK QUESTIONS** **EXERCISE 3:**

1. Do you have a mother?
2. Do you have a motorcycle?
3. Do you have a car?
4. Do you drive a motorcycle?
5. What is your name?
6. Do you like cars?

Yes, I have a mother.
Yes, I have a motorcycle.
Yes, I have a car.
Yes, I drive a motorcycle.
My name is _____.
Yes, I like cars.

PAGE 3 **ANSWERS TO THE WORKBOOK QUESTIONS** **EXERCISE 4:**

1. What does Raymond like to do?
2. What does Nancy like?
3. Who has a dog?
4. Where is Raymond's dog?
5. Is his dog friendly?
6. Do you like friendly dogs? (yes)
7. Do you like to drive a motorcycle? (yes)

He likes to drive his motorcycle.
She likes motorcycles and dogs.
Raymond has a dog.
It is outside.
Yes, it is friendly.
Yes, I like friendly dogs.
Yes, I like to drive a motorcycle.

PAGE 4 **ANSWERS TO THE STUDENT READER QUESTIONS** **ACTIVITY 4:**

1. Are they friends?
2. Is this a car?
3. Does he have a motorcycle?
4. Is this a dog?
5. Is he a policeman?
6. Is she a nurse?

Yes, they are friends.
Yes, this is a car.
Yes, he has a motorcycle.
Yes, this is a dog.
Yes, he is a policeman.
Yes, she is a nurse.

LESSON 2 CONTINUED

ACTIVITY 8:

Note to the teacher: Cut and distribute as outlined on Page 2 of this guide.
Tell the students to answer "yes" to all the questions as they haven't learned the negative format.

What is your name?   Do you have a mother?
My name is _____.   Yes, I have a mother.

Are you in English class?   Do you like cars?
Yes, I'm in English class.   Yes, I like cars.

Is your friend in English class?   Are your friends students?
Yes, my friend is in English class.   Yes, my friends are students.

Is a dog a friend?   Do you like motorcycles?
Yes, a dog is a friend.   Yes, I like motorcycles.

Do you have a pen?   Do you have a book?
Yes, I have a pen.   Yes, I have a book.

Are you a student?   Do you have a car?
Yes, I'm a student.   Yes, I have a car.

Are dogs friendly?   What is your teacher's name?
Yes, dogs are friendly.   My teacher's name is _____.

Do you have a friend?   Are your friends in this class?
Yes, I have a friend.   Yes, my friends are in this class.

Do you drive a motorcycle?   Do you drive a car?
Yes, I drive a motorcycle.   Yes, I drive a car.

Teacher Guide   6

LESSON 3

To the teacher:

- At this point the students have just had the negative for "to be", introduced in this lesson, but not the contractions.
They have not had the negative contractions for "to do".

ORAL QUESTIONS

Do you have a dog? (yes)	*Yes, I have a dog.*
Do you like pizza? (yes)	*Yes, I like pizza.*
Do you like Sprite? (yes)	*Yes, I like Sprite.*
Are you thirsty?	*Yes, I am thirsty.*
	No, I am not thirsty.
Are you outside?	*No, I am not outside.*
Are you a student?	*Yes, I'm a student.*
	No, I am not a student.
Are you a waiter?	*Yes, I am a waiter.*
	No, I am not a waiter.
Are you a waitress?	*Yes, I am a waitress.*
	No, I am not a waitress.
Are you cold?	*Yes, I am cold.*
	No, I am not cold.
Do you drink Sprite? (yes)	*Yes, I drink Sprite.*
Are you American?	*Yes, I am American.*
	No, I am not American.
Are you in an English class?	*Yes, I am in an English class.*
	No, I am not in an English class.
Are you hot?	*Yes, I am hot.*
	No, I am not hot.
Are you a student?	*Yes, I am a student.*
Do you want a glass of Sprite? (yes)	*Yes, I want a glass of Sprite.*
Do you like English class? (yes)	*Yes, I like English class.*

LESSON 3 CONTINUED

PAGE 4 ANSWERS TO THE WORKBOOK QUESTIONS **EXERCISE 1:**

1. Are you hot? *Yes, I am hot.*
   No, I am not hot.
2. Are you cold? *Yes, I am cold.*
   No, I am not cold.
3. Are you in a restaurant? *Yes, I am in a restaurant.*
   No, I am not in a restaurant.
4. Are you a waiter? *Yes, I am a waiter.*
   No, I am not a waiter.
5. Are you in an English class? *Yes, I am in an English class.*
6. Are you a teacher? *Yes, I am a teacher.*
   No, I'm not a teacher.
7. Are you outside? *No, I am not outside.*
8. Are you thirsty? *Yes, I am thirsty.*
   No, I am not thirsty.

PAGE 4 ANSWERS TO THE WORKBOOK QUESTIONS **EXERCISE 2:**

1. Do they have a dog? *Yes, they have a dog.*
2. Are they friends? *Yes, they are friends.*
3. Do they like pizza? *Yes, they like pizza.*
4. Are they in a restaurant? *Yes, they are in a restaurant.*
5. Is it a hamburger? *Yes it's a hamburger.*
6. Are they Canadian? *Yes, they are Canadian.*

PAGE 5 ANSWERS TO THE WORKBOOK QUESTIONS **EXERCISE 3:**

1. Does Nancy like to walk? *Yes, Nancy likes to walk.*
2. Does Peter like to walk? *Yes, Peter likes to walk.*
3. Does Nancy like to walk to class? *Yes, Nancy (she) likes to walk to class.*
4. Does Nancy have a car? *Yes, Nancy (she) has a car.*
5. Does Peter have a motorcycle? *Yes, Peter (he) has a motorcycle.*
6. Does Peter like to drive cars? *No, Peter does not like to drive cars.*
7. Do you like to drive cars? *Yes, I like to drive cars.*
   No, I do not like to drive cars.
8. What does Nancy like to drive? *She likes to drive motorcycles and cars.*

Note to the teacher: The Picture Bingo Activity introduces new nouns. The students will know some of them and the pictures will show the meanings of the others.

We understand that the students find using "to do" and "to be" difficult.

PICTURE BINGO

PAGES 10 - 23

To the teacher: Give a different card to each student. If there aren't enough different cards, then give the same card to two students who aren't sitting together.

Give each student a number of small objects such as beans or stones to place over the boxes as the words are called.

The teacher then calls the captions listed on the TEACHER'S COPY card in any order, allowing the students time to find the matching picture.
Help is given as the game is played, as the goal is for the students to hear the sentence captions many times. In this way they learn sentence word order as well as vocabulary.

The winner(s) of the game call BINGO when they have a straight and complete row of covered pictures. The covered rows can be in a straight vertical line, a straight horizontal line, or a straight diagonal line. The diagonal line must go from one corner to the other.

The FREE box is counted as a covered picture when it is a part of the completed row.

The game can be played a number of times until the students know the vocabulary well. At that point go to the **Enrichment Copy**, having the students use the same Bingo cards.

Call List

Use this randomly generated list as your call list when playing the game. There is no need to say the BINGO column name. Place some kind of mark (like an X, a checkmark, a dot, tally mark, etc) on each cell as you announce it, to keep track. You can also cut out each item, place them in a bag and pull words from the bag.

Call Outs

He buys a hot dog
He is wearing a blue shirt
He has a green pen They
have a blue bicycle He has
a phone
They have a big dog Her
car is blue
She walks with her dog She
buys a new dress They are
in a restaurant She rides a
horse
Her name is Julia

She has a baby
They are Canadians
They often eat pizza
He drives a motorcycle
They have some juice
She sits on a chair
She can go fast on her roller blades
It is a red truck
They walk together
She has a green shirt
They are in love
They shake hands

BINGO **TEACHER'S COPY ENRICHMENT**

She is a mother
They live in Canada
They like pizza
He has a motorcycle
They drink juice
She sits
She has roller blades
It is a red truck
They walk
She has 7 books
They kiss
They meet

He likes hot dogs
He has a blue shirt
It is his pen
It is his bicycle
He walks
They have a dog
She drives a blue car
It is her dog
She has a dress
They are in a restaurant
She has a horse
She is Julia

B I N G O

Free!

B I N G O

Free!

B I N G O

Free!

B I N G O

Free!

B I N G O

Free!

B I N G O

Free!

B I N G O

BINGO

Free!

B I N G O

Free!

B I N G O

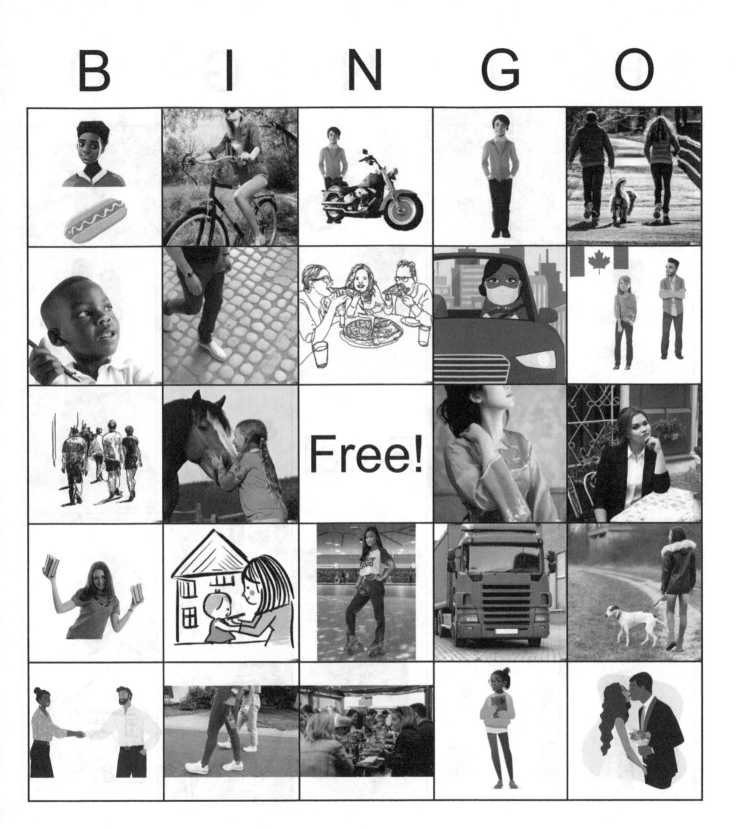

B I N G O

		Free!		

B I N G O

Free!

B I N G O

Free!

B I N G O

B I N G O

B I N G O

LESSON 4

To the teacher: Although we try to avoid introducing new material in the Test Lessons, Lesson 4 has several new concepts. You may want to delay giving the test until the next class.

ORAL QUESTIONS
Review the oral questions in Lessons 1 to 3.
The students find the negative use of "to do" quite difficult but extensive oral practice will help them to make their responses automatic.

Do you have a brother?

Yes, I have a brother.
No, I don't have a brother.

Now turn to another student and ask:

Does he / she have a brother?

Yes, he / she has a brother.
No, he she doesn't have a brother.

Continue in the same way with these questions.

Do you have a dog?

Yes, I have a dog.
No, I don't have a dog.

Does he / she have a dog.

Yes, he / she has a dog.
No, he / she doesn't have a dog.

Continue using car, motorcycle, friend, drink, book, pen.

PAGE 6   ANSWERS TO THE WORKBOOK QUESTIONS   EXERCISE 1:

1. Are they in an English class? (yes)   *Yes, they're in English class.*
2. Is he in a restaurant? (yes)   *Yes, he's in a restaurant.*
3. Are you in England?   *Yes, I'm in England.*
                                                     No, I'm not in England.
4. Are you thirsty?   *Yes, I'm thirsty.*
                                                     No, I am not thirsty.
5. Is it cold today?   *Yes, it's cold today.*
                                                     No, it isn't cold today.
6. Are we waiters? (yes)   *Yes, we're waiters.*
7. Is this your dog?   *Yes, it's my dog.*
    No, it isn't my dog.
8. Are they your friends? (yes)   *Yes, they're my friends.*

PAGE 6   ANSWERS TO THE WORKBOOK QUESTIONS   EXERCISE 2:
Answer in sentences using a contraction of "to do"

1. Do you have a car? (no)   *No, I don't have a car.*
2. Does your friend drink Sprite? (no)   *No, my friend doesn't drink Sprite.*
3. Do you want a drink? (no)   *No, I don't want a drink*
4. Do you like motorcycles? (no)   *No, I don't like motorcycles.*
5. Do you have a dog? (no)   *No, I don't have a dog.*
6. Do you like pizza? (no)   *No, I don't like pizza.*
7. Does your friend drive a car? (no)   *No, my friend doesn't drive a car.*
8. Do you have a glass of Sprite? (no)   *No, I don't have a glass of Sprite.*
9. Does your friend have a motorcycle? (no)   *No, my friend doesn't have a motorcycle.*

Teacher Guide   27

LESSON 4 CONTINUED

ACTIVITY 2:

Cut and distribute as outlined on Page 2 of this Guide.

Do you drink _____ juice?
Yes, I drink _____ juice.
No, I don't drink _____ juice.

Are you cold?
Yes, I'm cold.
No, I'm not cold.

Are you Canadian?
Yes, I'm Canadian.
No, I'm not Canadian.

Are you an English student?
Yes, I'm an English student.

Do you have a dog?
Yes, I have a dog.
No, I don't have a dog.

Do you drink juice?
Yes, I drink juice.
No, I don't drink juice.

Are you thirsty?
Yes, I'm thirsty.
No, I'm not thirsty.

Do you have a friend?
Yes, I have a friend.
No, I don't have a friend.

Do your friends drive cars?
Yes, my friends drive cars.
No, my friends don't drive cars.

Are you a waitress?
Yes, I'm a waitress.
No, I'm not a waitress.

Do you like dogs?
Yes, I like dogs.
No, I don't like dogs.

Is it hot today?
Yes, it's hot today.
No, it's not hot today.

Are you a teacher?
Yes, I'm a teacher.
No, I'm not a teacher.

Do you like hamburgers?
Yes, I like hamburgers.
No, I don't like hamburgers.

Is it cold in your city?
Yes, it's cold in our city.
No, it isn't cold in our city.

Do you like cats?
Yes, I like cats.
No, I don't like cats.

Do you like pizza?
Yes, I like pizza.
No, I don't like pizza.

Do you have a car?
Yes, I have a car.
No, I don't have a car.

Teacher Guide

28

LESSON 4 CONTINUED

ANSWERS TO THE TEST QUESTIONS

1. *Yes, I drive a car. / No, I don't drive a car.*
2. *Yes, I drink juice. / No, I don't drink juice.*
3. *Yes, they have a dog.*
4. *Yes, I like pizza. / No. I don't like pizza.*
5. *Yes, they have a glass of juice.*
6. *Yes, they are friends.*
7. *Yes, I drink juice with my friends.*   v
   No, I don't drink juice with my friends.

Complete the dialogue. (1 mark each)

8. Tom: What *is* your name?   **9. Carol:** My name *is* Carol.
10. Tom: *Are* you from Tibet?   **11. Carol:** Yes, **I** *am* / I'm *not* from Tibet.
12. Tom: *Are* you a teacher?   **13. Carol:** No, I *am* / **I'm** not a teacher.
14. Tom: *Is* Maria your friend?   **15. Carol:** Yes, she *is* my friend.
16. Tom: *Are* they students?   **17. Carol:** Yes, they *are* students.

Write the sentences with contractions.   (2 marks each)

18. **She is Carol.**   ***She's Carol.***

19. They are teachers.   ***They're*** teachers.
20. I am hot.   ***I'm*** hot.
21. He is your friend.   ***He's*** your friend.
22. We are in English class.   ***We're*** in English class.
23. It is a glass of juice.   ***It's*** a glass of juice.

Teacher Guide   29

TEST 1   LESSONS 1 TO 4   NAME: _____

Answer in sentences. (4 marks each)

1. Do you drive a car?_____

2. Do you drink juice? _____

3. Do they have a dog? _____

4. Do you like pizza? _____

5. Do they have a glass of juice? _____

6. Are they friends?   _____

7. Do you drink juice with your friends?   _____

Complete the sentences. (1 mark each)

8. **Tom:**   What _____ your name?

9. **Carol:** My name _____ Carol.

10. **Tom:**   _____ you from Tibet?

11. **Carol:** Yes, I _____ from Tibet.

12. **Tom:**   _____ you a teacher?

13. **Carol:** No, I _____ not a teacher.

14. **Tom:**   _____ Maria your friend?

15. **Carol:** Yes, she _____ my friend.

16. **Tom:**   _____ they students?

17. **Carol:** Yes, they _____ students.

Write the sentences with contractions.   (2 marks each)

EXAMPLE: It is hot.   It's hot.

18. She is Carol.   _____

19. They are teachers.   _____

20. I am hot.   _____

21. He is your friend.   _____

22. We are in English class.   _____

23. It is a glass of juice.   _____

ESSON 5
ORAL QUESTIONS

To the teacher: Ask these questions, pointing to different students as you use the possessive adjectives introduced in Lesson 2.

Is this your pen?	*Yes, it is my pen.*
Is this my pen?	*Yes, it is your pen.*
Is this his pen?	*Yes, it is his pen.*
Is this her pen?	*Yes, it is her pen.*
Are these their pens? (yes)	*Yes, they are their pens.*
Am I your teacher?	*Yes, you are my teacher.*
Are you his friend?	*Yes, I am his friend.*
Are you her friend?	*Yes, I am her friend.*
What is his name?	*His name is _____.*
What is her name?	*Her name is _____.*
Whose pen is this?	*It is my pen.*
Whose book is this?	*It is _____ (Jim's) book.*
	It is my / his / her / book.
Is he your friend?	*Yes, he is my friend.*

Do you eat pasta?	*Yes, I eat pasta.*
	No, I don't eat pasta.
Do you like hamburgers?	*Yes, I like hamburgers.*
	No, I don't like hamburgers.
Do you sometimes eat in a restaurant?	*Yes, I sometimes eat in a restaurant.*
	No, I don't eat in a restaurant.
Do you order hamburgers in a restaurant?	*Yes, I order hamburgers in a restaurant.*
	No, I don't order hamburgers in a restaurant.
Do you drink apple juice?	*Yes, I drink apple juice.*
	No, I don't drink apple juice.
Do you make mistakes?	*No, I don't make mistakes.*
	Yes, I make mistakes.
Do you have a book?	*Yes, I have a book.*
	No, I don't have a book.
Do you like chicken?	*Yes, I like chicken.*
	No, I don't like chicken.
Do you meet your friends in class?	*Yes, I meet my friends in class.*
	No, I don't meet my friends in class.

LESSON 5 CONTINUED

1. Where are the friends?   The friends are in a restaurant.
2. What do they do?   They order in a restaurant.
3. Does Carol like pasta?   Yes, Carol likes pasta.
4. Does Tom like hamburgers?   Yes, Tom likes hamburgers.
5. Does Carol like apple juice?   No, Carol doesn't like apple juice.
6. Does Sarah like chicken?   Yes, Sarah likes chicken.
7. Does Sarah like hamburgers?   No, Sarah doesn't like hamburgers.
8. Does Peter like pizza?   Yes, Peter likes pizza.

1. What does Sarah order?   *Sarah orders chicken.*
2. What does Carol order?   *Carol orders pasta.*
3. What does Peter order?   *Peter orders pizza.*
4. Do you eat in a restaurant?   *Yes, I eat in a restaurant.*
                                 No, I don't eat in a restaurant.
5. What do you order?   *I order _____.*
6. What does your friend order? *My friend orders _____.*
7. Do you make pasta?   *Yes, I make pasta.*
                                 No, I don't make pasta.
8. Do you make hamburgers?   *Yes, I make hamburgers.*
                                 No, I don't make hamburgers.
9. Do you drink apple juice?   *Yes, I drink apple juice.*
                                 No, I don't drink apple juice.

Carol, Tom, *Peter* and Sarah are in the *restaurant*. Carol orders *pasta*. Tom doesn't like *pasta*. He orders *hamburgers*. Peter orders *pizza*.
They *all* want something to drink. They order *mango juice*. The waiter makes *mistakes*. The four friends *correct* his mistakes.

hamburgers   *you eat them*
restaurant   *you eat there*
juice   *you drink it*
a friend   *you like him or her*
a glass   *you put something to drink in it*
cold   *not hot*
thirsty   *you want something to drink*
to drive   *to make a car go*

LESSON 6

ORAL QUESTIONS

What is your last name?	*My last name is* _____.
What is your middle name?	*My middle name is* _____.
What is your surname?	*My surname is* _____.
What is your full name?	*My full name is* _____.

PAGE 9   **ANSWERS TO THE WORKBOOK QUESTIONS**   **EXERCISE 1:**

1. *I __am__ a student.*
2. *They __are__ students.*
3. *We __are__ inside.*
4. *He __is__ a teacher.*
5. *She __is__ my friend.*
6. *You __are__ a student.*

PAGE 9   **ANSWERS TO THE WORKBOOK QUESTIONS**   **EXERCISE 2:**

1. Are you in town? (no)   *No, I'm not in town.*
2. Are we in a restaurant? (no)   *No, we aren't in a restaurant.*
3. Are they Chinese? (no)   *No, they aren't Chinese.*
4. Are you American? (no)   *No, I'm not American.*
5. Is your friend a teacher? (no)   *No, my friend isn't a teacher.*
6. Are they dogs?   *No, they aren't dogs.*

PAGE 9   **ANSWERS TO THE WORKBOOK QUESTIONS**   **EXERCISE 3:**

surname	*last name*
first	*number 1*
chicken	*you eat it*
plural	*more than one*
classmates	*students in your class*
mango juice	*you drink it*
waitress	*she is in a restaurant*
glass	*you have something to drink in it*

PAGE 10   **ANSWERS TO THE WORKBOOK QUESTIONS**   **EXERCISE 4:**

1. *Emily's full name is Emily Jane Prescott*
2. *Her first name is Emily.*
3. *Her middle name is Jane.*
4. *Her last name is Prescott.*
5. *My first name is* _____.
6. *My surname is* _____.
7. *My full name is* _____.

LESSON 6 CONTINUED

PAGE 10   ANSWERS TO THE WORKBOOK QUESTIONS   EXERCISE 5:

1. *Yes, David is a student.*
2. *Yes, Susan is David's friend.*
3. *Yes, Susan is a student.*

4. *Yes, I am a student (too).*
5. *Yes, I study English.*
6. *Yes, I study Spanish, too.*
7. *No, I don't study Spanish, too.*

ACTIVITY 6:

Appendix 1:

You'll find the pictures for this activity (Fish) in Appendix 1 at the end of this Guide.

FISH

Divide the students into groups of three.   (one group of four if necessary)
Copy two sets of cards for each group of students.   Have the students deal out all the cards.

If they have any pairs of pictures, they are to exchange them with others in their group.

First player: *Do you have a _____?*
Any other player: *Yes, I have a _____.*   *No, I don't have a _____.*

The student who has it takes the card and puts it on the table with the one in his / her hand.

OR

Divide the students into groups of two. (One group of three for an uneven number.)
Place all the cards face down on the table.
The students are to take turns picking up a card.
If they know the name, they keep the card, if not then it is put at the bottom of the pile.

OR

Play the Memory Game

Spread the cards face down in rows. Take turns to turn over two cards.
If the cards match and the player can name them, then he / she keeps them.
If not, then they are replaced face down on the table.

LESSON 7 ORAL QUESTIONS

Do the Carters have a dog?   *Yes, the Carters have a dog.*
What is the dog's name?   *The dog's name is Toto.*
Who are Ruth's mother and father?   *Ruth's mother and father are*
Jessica and Craig *Carter.*

Who is Raymond?   *Raymond is* Craig *and Jessica*
Carter's son.
Who is Craig's daughter?   *Craig's daughter is Ruth.*
What is Craig's son's name?   *Craig's son's name is Raymond.*

Who is Raymond's mother?   *Raymond's mother is Jessica Carter.*
Who is Jessica's daughter?   *Jessica's daughter is Ruth.*
Who is Ruth's father?   *Craig is Ruth's father.*

What is Ruth's mother's name?   *Ruth's mother's name is Jessica.*
What is your name?   *My name is _____.*
What is the family's surname?   *Their surname is Carter.*

Who is Craig and Jessica's daughter?   *Their daughter is Ruth.*
Who is Craig and Jessica's son?   *Their son is Raymond.*
Who is the father in the family?   *Craig is the father in the family.*

Who is the mother in the family?   *Jessica is the mother in the family.*
Do you have a brother?   *Yes, I have a brother.*
         No, I don't have a brother.
Do you have a sister?   *Yes, I have a sister.*
         No, I don't have a sister.

Do Craig and Jessica have a son?   *Yes, they have a son.*
Do Craig and Jessica have a daughter?   *Yes, they have a daughter.*

Whose daughter is Ruth?   *Ruth is Craig and Jessica daughter.*
Is Raymond Jessica's son?   *Yes, Raymond is Jessica's son.*
Is Raymond Craig's son?   *Yes, Raymond is Craig's son.*

Whose son is Raymond?   *Raymond is Craig and Jessica's son.*
Do the Carters have a dog?   *Yes, the Carters have a dog.*
What is their dog's name?   *Its name is Toto.*

Do you walk in town?   *Yes, I walk in town.*
         No, I don't walk in town.
Do you have a dog?   *Yes, I have a dog.*
         No, I don't have a dog.
Are dogs friendly?   *Yes, dogs are friendly.*
         No, dogs aren't friendly.

LESSON 7 CONTINUED

PAGE 11 **ANSWERS TO THE WORKBOOK QUESTIONS** **EXERCISE 1:**

1. They aren't students.
2. We aren't in town.
3. He isn't a teacher.
4. They aren't friends.
5. It isn't a dog.

PAGE 11 **ANSWERS TO THE WORKBOOK QUESTIONS** **EXERCISE 2:**

1. Yes, the Carter family has a daughter.
2. Yes, the Carter family has a son.
3. Yes, the Carter family has a mother.
4. Yes, the Carter family has a father.
5. Yes, they have a dog.
6. Yes, I have a dog. / No, I don't have a dog.

PAGE 11 **ANSWERS TO THE WORKBOOK QUESTIONS** **EXERCISE 3:**

1. Are Raymond and George friends? *Yes, they are friends.*
2. How is Jennifer? *She's fine.*
3. What is Jennifer learning? *She's learning English.*
4. Does Jennifer have brothers? *Yes, she has two brothers.*
5. Does she have a sister? *No, she doesn't have a sister.*
6. Who says "Have a good day"? *Raymond says, "Have a good day".*
7. Do you have brothers and sisters? *Yes, I have _____.*

PAGE 12 **ANSWERS TO THE WORKBOOK QUESTIONS** **EXERCISE 4:**

1. *A shoe is in box number two.*
2. *A cup is in box number eleven.*
3. *A tie is in box number six.*
4. *A window is in box number one.*
5. *A blouse is in box number three.*
6. *A T-shirt is in box number twelve.*
7. *A jacket is in box number five.*
8. *A cat is in box number ten.*
9. *A house is in box number nine.*
10. *A bird is in box number four.*
11. *A hat is in box number seven.*
12. *A door is in box number eight.*

Teacher Guide

LESSON 7 CONTINUED

PAGE 12 **ANSWERS TO THE WORKBOOK QUESTIONS** **EXERCISE 5:**

family	*mother, father, son, daughter*
son	*a mother and father's boy*
daughter	*a mother and father's girl*
fine	*good*
How do you do?	*formal introduction*
Nice to meet you.	*informal introduction*
tea	*a hot drink*
mine	*it's yours*
cup	*you drink from it*

PAGE 13 **ANSWERS TO THE WORKBOOK QUESTIONS** **EXERCISE 6:**

David is from Canada. He is ***Canadian.*** He has a friend. Her name is Mary.
She is Canadian. She's from ***Canada*** . David has a motorcycle. He likes ***motorcycles***.
Mary has a car. She doesn't drive a motorcycle. She likes to ***drive*** her car to the city.
Sometimes she goes to the ***church***. David drives his motorcycle to ***school***. He studies
English. Mary likes Canada. She wants to study ***Canadian*** history.

PAGE 13 **ANSWERS TO THE WORKBOOK QUESTIONS** **EXERCISE 7:**

1.	Is Mary a boy or a girl?	*Mary is a girl.*
2.	Where is David from?	*He is from Canada.*
3.	Where is Mary from?	*She is from Canada.*
4.	Does Mary have a motorcycle?	*No, she doesn't have a motorcycle.*
5.	Where does Mary like to drive?	*She likes to drive to the city.*
6.	What does Mary want to study	*She wants to study Canadian history.*

ACTIVITY 5:   TEAM QUESTIONS

Do you have a daughter?
Yes, I have a daughter.
No, I don't have a daughter.

Do you like restaurants?
Yes, I like restaurants.
No, I don't like restaurants.

Does your mother have a car?
Yes, my mother has a car.
No, my mother doesn't have a car.

Does your friend live in Canada?
Yes, my friend lives in Canada.
No, my friend doesn't live in Canada.

Does your dog eat pasta?
Yes, my dog eats pasta.
No, my dog doesn't eat pasta.

Does your cat eat hamburgers?
Yes, my cat eats hamburgers.
No, my cat doesn't eat hamburgers.

Does your brother drive a motorcycle?
Yes, my brother drives a motorcycle.
No, my brother doesn't drive a motorcycle.

Does your sister drive a car?
Yes, my sister drives a car.
No, my sister doesn't drive a car.

Do you eat hamburgers?
Yes, I eat hamburgers.
No, I don't eat hamburgers.

Does your friend live in Canada?
Yes, my friend lives in Canada.
No, my friend doesn't live in Canada.

Are you a waiter?
Yes, I am a waiter.
No, I am not a waiter.

Do you make mistakes?
Yes, I make mistakes.
No, I don't make mistakes.

Does your dog eat chicken?
Yes, my dog eats chicken.
No, my dog doesn't eat chicken.

Does your friend have a dog?
Yes, my friend has a dog.
No, my friend doesn't have a dog.

Does your father have four sisters?
Yes, my father has four sisters.
No, my father doesn't have four sisters.

Does your mother have two brothers.
Yes, my mother has two brothers.
No, my mother doesn't have two brothers.

Does your friend drink mango juice?
Yes, my friend drinks mango juice.
No, my friend doesn't drink mango juice.

How are you?
I'm fine.

LESSON 8   REVIEW
ORAL QUESTIONS
Have the students answer in sentences.

Whose book is this?   *It is my book. It is _____'s book.*

Is she a teacher?   *Yes, she is (she's) a teacher.*
                                  No, she is not a teacher.

Who are they?   *They are (they're) _____ and _____.*

Are they students?   *Yes, they are students.*
                                  No, they are not students.

What is his name?   *His name is _____.*

What are their names?   *Their names are _____ and _____.*

What is your friend's name?   *His / her name is _____.*

_____, this is _____.   *Hello _____, nice to meet you.*

Do you have a book?   *Yes, I have a book.*

Whose pen is this?   *It is my pen. It is _____'s pen.*

What is your first name?   *My first name is _____.*

What is your middle name?   *My middle name is _____.*

What is your last name?   *My last name is _____.*

What is your full name?   *My full name is _____.*

Who comes to English class?   *_____ comes to English class.*

Does your house have a window?   *Yes, my house has a window.*
                                  Yes, our house has a window.

Does your house have a door?   *Yes, my house has a door.*
                                  Yes, our house has a door.

Do you have a daughter?   *Yes, I have a daughter.*
                                  No, I do not (don't) have a daughter.

Do you come to English class?   *Yes, I come to English class.*

Does your father have a son?   *Yes, my father has a son.*
                                  No, my father does not (doesn't) have a son.

Does your mother have a daughter?   *Yes, my mother has a daughter.*
                                  No, my mother does not (doesn't) have a
daughter.

Does your mother have a cat?   *Yes, my mother has a cat.*
                                  No, my mother does not (doesn't) have a cat.

Does your father have a dog?   *Yes, my father has a dog.*
                                  No, my father does not (doesn't) have a dog.

Do you live in Paris?   *Yes, I live in Paris.*
                                  No, I don't live in Paris.

LESSON 8 CONTINUED

PAGE 14   ANSWERS TO THE WORKBOOK QUESTIONS   EXERCISE 1:

1. *It is a window.*   2. *It is a bird.*   3. *Yes, I have a tie./ No, I don't have a…*
4. *It is a cup.*   5. *Yes, I have a cat. No, I don't have a cat.*   6. *It is a house.*
7. *Yes, it is a jacket* 8. *Yes, it is a shoe.*   9. *Yes, a house has a door.*
10. *Yes, they are friends.*   11. *Yes, she has a daughter.*   12. *Yes, they meet.*
13. *Yes, he has a son.*   14. *It is a hat.*

PAGES 15 AND 16   ANSWERS TO THE WORKBOOK QUESTIONS EXERCISES 2 / 1:

1. *The Carter's dog's name is Toto.*
2. *Yes, Craig has a son and a daughter.*
3. *Yes, Jessica has a daughter.*
4. *Craig's son's name is Raymond.*
5. *Raymond's mother is Jessica.*
6. *Jessica's daughter is Ruth.*
7. *Yes, I have a dog. /No, I don't have a dog.*
8. *Yes I have a son. / No, I don't have a son.*
9. *Yes, I have a daughter. / No, I don't have a daughter.*
10. *Yes, I have a sister. / No, I don't have a sister.*
11. *Yes, I have a brother. / No, I don't have a brother.*
12. *Yes, I live in town. / No, I don't live in town.*

1. *Does she have a hamburger?*
2. *Are they in English class?*
3. *Does he meet a friend?*
4. *Do they walk in town?*
5. *Is his last name Carter?*
6. *Do the Carters have a dog?*
7. *Do you like coffee?*

PAGE 17   ANSWERS TO THE STUDENT READER QUESTIONS   ACTIVITY 1:

1. *Yes, I'm an English student.*
2. *Yes, it is my book.*
   No, it isn't my book.
3. *Yes, my house has a window.*
4. *Yes, I have a daughter.*
   No, I don't have a daughter.
5. *My first name is _____.*
6. *Yes, my mother has a dog.*
   No, my mother doesn't have a dog.
7. *Yes, I study English.*

8. *My surname is _____.*
9. *Yes, I have a friend.*
   No, I don't have a friend.
10. *No, I'm not in my house.*
11. *Yes, my father has a son.*
    No, my father doesn't have a son.
12. *My friend's name is _____.*
13. *Yes, my father has a tie.*
    No, my father doesn't have a tie.
14. *My last name is _____.*

PAGE 17   ANSWERS TO THE STUDENT READER QUESTIONS   ACTIVITY 3:

1. *Yes, I have five sisters.*
   No, I don't have five sisters.
2. *Yes, I have a son.*
   No, I don't have a son.
3. *Yes, I meet my friend in town.*
   No, I don't meet my friend in town.
4. *Yes, I have three brothers.*
   No, I don't have three brothers.
5. *Yes, I like hamburgers./ No, I don't like…*
6. *Yes, I study French.*

7. *Yes, I eat pizza.*
   No, I don't eat pizza.
8. *Yes, I have a hat.*
   No, I don't have a hat.
9. *Yes, I walk in town.*
   No, I don't walk in town.
10. *Yes, I live in a town.*
    No, I don't live in a town.
11. *Yes, I live in Canada. / No, I don't…*
12. *Yes, I have a daughter. / No I don't…*

LESSON 8 CONTINUED

TEST 2 TOTAL MARKS: 50

ORAL QUESTIONS FOR TEST 2

1. What is your surname?

2. Are you an English student?

3. Do you have a bird?

4. Does your father have a dog?

5. Does your house have a door?

ORAL QUESTION ANSWERS (4 marks each)

1. *My surname is _____.*

2. *Yes, I am (I'm) an English student.*

3. *Yes, I have a bird.*
   No, I do not (don't) have a bird.

4. *Yes, my father has a dog.*
   No, my father does not (doesn't) have a dog.

5. *Yes, my house has a door.*

NOTE:

The students may answer the oral questions on the test in writing,
or individually with the teacher.

ANSWERS TO TEST 2

COMPLETE USING THE CORRECT FORM OF THE VERB. (1 mark each)

to be

6. I *am* a student.
7. They *are* in town.
8. She *is* a friend.
9. We *are* students.

to have

10. He *has* a dog.
11. You *have* a T-shirt.

to walk

12. She *walks* to English class.

to meet

13. He *meets* her sometimes.

to do

14. They (*do* not) (don't) come to class.
15. She (*does* not) (doesn't) meet him.

ANSWER THE QUESTIONS IN SENTENCES. (4 marks each)

16. What is your friend's surname?
17. What is your full name?
18. Do you walk to class?

19. Is pasta good for you?

20. Do you have a jacket?

My friend's surname is _____.
My full name is _____.
Yes, I walk to class.
No, I don't walk to class.
Yes, pasta is good for you.
No, pasta is not (isn't) good for you.
Yes, I have a jacket.
No, I don't have a jacket.

LESSONS 5 TO 8 TEST 2 NAME:_____

Answer in sentences (4 marks each)

1. _____

2. _____

3. _____

4. _____

5. _____

Complete using the correct form of the verb. (1 mark each)

to be

6. I _____ a student.

7. They_____ in town.

8. She _____ a friend.

9. We _____ students.

to have

10. He _____ a dog.

11. You _____ a T-shirt.

to walk

12. She _____ to English class.

to meet

13. He _____ her sometimes.

to do

14. They _____ not come to class.

15. She _____ not meet him.

Answer the questions in sentences. (4 marks each)

16. What is your friend's surname?

_____

17. What is your full name?

_____

18. Do you walk to class?

_____

19. Is pasta good for you?

_____

20. Do you have a jacket?

_____

LESSON 9 ORAL QUESTIONS

Do you have a daughter?

Yes, I have a daughter?
No, I don't have a daughter.

Now go to another student and ask this next question as you point to the student you just asked.

Does he / she have a daughter?

Yes, he / she has a daughter.
No, he / she doesn't have a daughter.

Do you have a son in _____? (country)

Yes, I have a son in _____.
No, I don't have a son in _____.

Go to another student as explained above.
Does he / she have a son in _____?

Yes, he / she has a son in _____.
No, he / she doesn't have a son in _____.

Continue in this way to give the students practice using "don't" and "doesn't"

Do you have a sister in _____ (city)?

Yes, I have a sister in _____.
No, I don't have a sister in _____.

Does he / she have a sister?

Yes, he / she has a sister.
No, he / she doesn't have a sister.

Do you have a brother in ____ (country)?

Yes, I have a brother in _____.
No, I don't have a brother in _____.

Does he / she have a brother?

Yes, he / she has a brother.
No, he / she doesn't have a brother.

Do you have a wife?

Yes, I have a wife.
No, I don't have a wife.

Does he have a wife?

Yes, he has a wife.
No, he doesn't have a wife.

Do you have a husband?

Yes, I have a husband.
No, I don't have a husband.

Does she have a husband?

Yes, she has a husband.
No, she doesn't have a husband.

Do you like mango juice?

Yes, I like mango juice.
No, I don't like mango juice.

Does he / she like mango juice?

Yes, he / she likes mango juice.
No, he / she doesn't like mango juice.

Is John a boy?

Yes, John is a boy.

LESSON 9 CONTINUED`

PAGE 16   QUESTIONS FOR THE WORKBOOK SENTENCES   EXERCISE 1:

1. She has a hamburger.   *Does she have a hamburger?*
                                                  What does she have?

2. They are in English class.   *Are they in English class?*
3. He meets a friend.   *Does he meet a friend?*
4. They walk to town.   *Do they walk to town?*
                                                  Where do they walk?

5. His last name is Carter.   *What is his last name?*
6. Yes, the Carters have a dog.   *Do the Carters have a dog?*
7. No, I don't like coffee.   *Do you like coffee?*

PAGE 16   ANSWERS TO THE WORKBOOK QUESTIONS   EXERCISE 2:

1. Yes, my name is Dale. / No, my name isn't Dale. 2. Yes, I have a cat. / No, I don't have a cat.
3. No, the Carter family isn't French.   4. No, Ruth Carter doesn't have a bird.
5. Yes, I have a dog. / No, I don't have a dog.   6. Yes, I'm a student.
7. Yes, they are in the town.   8. Yes, Craig Carter has a son.
9. Yes, I am learning English.

PAGE 17   ANSWERS TO THE WORKBOOK QUESTIONS   EXERCISE 3:

1. My friend's name is ___ . / I don't have a friend.   2. My mother's first name is _____ .
3. My father's last name is _____ .   4. My brother's name is _____ . / I don't...
5. My sister's name is _____ ./ I don't have a sister.   6. My grandmother's name is ___ . I don't...
7. My grandfather's name is _____ .   8. Yes, it's his book./No, it's not his book.

PAGE 17   ANSWERS TO THE WORKBOOK QUESTIONS   EXERCISE 4:

Susan and John go to John's grandparents' *house*. Susan meets his grandparents, Mr.
and *Mrs.* Johnson. They are *pleased* to meet her. They all *shake* hands.
Grandfather is *thirsty*. He needs a cup of *tea*. Mrs. Johnson, John's
grandmother, says she is *hot*. She wants to have a *glass* of cold mango juice.

LESSON 9 CONTINUED

PAGE 18   ANSWERS TO THE WORKBOOK QUESTIONS   ACTIVITY 3:

1.   *Yes, he / she has a window in his / her house.*
       No, he / she doesn't have a window in his / her house.
2.   *Yes, he / she has two shoes.*
3.   *Yes, she has a husband. / No, she doesn't have a husband.*
4.   *Yes, he / she has a bird in his / her house.*
       No, he / she doesn't have a bird in his / her house.
5.   *Yes, he has a wife. / No, he doesn't have a wife.*
6.   *Yes, he / she has a sister. / No, he / she doesn't have a sister.*
7.   *Yes, he / she has a door in his / her house.*
8.   *Yes, he / she has a brother. / No, he / she doesn't have a brother.*
9.   *Yes, he / she is in town. / No, he / she isn't in town.*

PAGE 18   Note to the teacher:

John introduces his grandparents formally as Mr. and Mrs. because they are older and meeting for the first time. At first, Susan will call them Mr. and Mrs. Johnson, but after a little while they will tell her what they like to be called.

This kind of formal introduction is changing very quickly. John might have introduced them by their first names. Susan might continue to use their formal names until she marries John.

PAGE 18   ANSWERS TO THE WORKBOOK QUESTIONS   EXERCISE 5:

1.   *Yes, she meets them for the first time.* 2.   *Yes, John's grandfather likes tea.*
3.   *Yes, they are pleased to meet Susan.*   4.   *She has a cup of tea.*
I like _____ to drink.

LESSON 10 ORAL QUESTIONS

Where are you from?   *I'm from _____. (country or city)*
Are you from _____?   *Yes, I'm from _____.*
                                             No, I'm not from _____.

Do you have a son in _____ (country)?   *Yes, I have a son in _____.*
                                             No, I don't have a son in _____.

Now go to another student and ask this next question as you point to the student you just asked.

Does he / she have a son in _____(country)? *Yes, he / she has a son in _____.*
                                             No, he / she doesn't have a son in _____.

Do you have a sister in ____ (city)?   *Yes, I have a sister in _____.*
                                             No, I don't have a sister in _____.

Does he / she have a sister in ___ (country)? *Yes, he / she has a sister in _____.*
                                             No, he / she doesn't have a sister in _____.

Do you have a brother in ___ (country)?   *Yes, I have a brother in _____.*
                                             No, I don't have a brother in _____.

Does he / she have a brother in _____?   *Yes, he / she has a brother in _____.*
                                             No, he / she doesn't have a brother in _____.

Do you have a daughter in ____? (city)   *Yes, I have a daughter in _____.*
                                             No, I don't have a daughter in _____.

Does he /she have a daughter in _____?   *Yes, he / she has a daughter in _____.*
                                             No, he / she doesn't have a daughter in _____.

Is your grandfather from ___ (country)?   *Yes, my grandfather is from _____.*
                                             No, my grandfather isn't from _____.

Is your grandmother from ___ (city)?   *Yes, my grandmother is from _____.*
                                             No, my grandmother isn't from _____.

Is your wife from _____ (city)?   *Yes, my wife is from _____.*
                                             No, my wife isn't from _____.
                                             I don't have a wife.

Is your husband from _____ (city)?   *Yes, my husband is from _____.*
                                             No, my husband isn't from _____.
                                             I don't have a husband.

Does your grandmother come from Spain?   *Yes, my grandmother comes from Spain.*
                                             No, my grandmother doesn't come from Spain.

Does his /her grandmother come from Spain?   *Yes, his/her grandmother comes from Spain.*
                                             No, his/her grandmother doesn't come from Spain.

Teacher Guide

LESSON 10 CONTINUED

PAGE 19   **ANSWERS TO THE WORKBOOK QUESTIONS**   **ACTIVITY 2:**

1. Where are you from?   *He's / She's from _____.*
2. Are you English?   *No, he's/she's not English.*
3. Are you from Russia?   *Yes, he's /she's from Russia.*
                                          No, he's / she's not from Russia.
4. Where is your mother from?   *She's _____*
5. Where is your father from?   *He's _____*

PAGE 19   **ANSWERS TO THE WORKBOOK QUESTIONS**   **ACTIVITY 3:**

1. Does she have a cat?   *Yes, she has a cat.*   *No, she doesn't have a cat.*
2. Does he have a dog?   *Yes, he has a dog.*   *No, he doesn't have a dog.*
3. Does he have a car?   *Yes, he has a car.*   *No, he doesn't have a car.*
4. Does she have a Sprite?   *Yes, she has a Sprite.*   *No, she doesn't have a Sprite.*
5. Do they have a pen?   *Yes, they have a pen.*   *No, they don't have a pen.*
6. Does he have a jacket?   *Yes, he has a jacket.*   *No, he doesn't have a jacket.*
7. Does she have a notebook? *Yes, she has a notebook.* *No, she doesn't have a notebook.*
8. Does she have a book?   *Yes, she has a book.*   *No, she doesn't have a book.*
9. Do they have juice?   *Yes, they have juice.*   *No, they don't have juice.*
10. Does she have a bird?   *Yes, she has a bird.*   *No, she doesn't have a bird.*

PAGE 20   **ANSWERS TO THE WORKBOOK QUESTIONS**   **EXERCISE 1:**

1. Do the Carters have a cat?   *No, the Carters don't have a cat.*
2. Does Ruth have a son? (no)   *No, Ruth doesn't have a son.*
3. Does Craig Carter have a daughter?   *Yes, Craig Carter has a daughter.*
4. Does Raymond have a grandfather? (no) *No, Raymond doesn't have a grandfather.*
5. Does Jessica have a grandmother? (no) *No, Jessica doesn't have a grandmother.*
6. Does Craig have a sister? (no)   *No, Craig does not (doesn't) have a sister.*
7. Does Raymond have a brother? (no)   *No, Raymond does not (doesn't) have a brother.*
8. Does Ruth have a friend? (yes)   *Yes, Ruth has a friend.*
9. Does the Carter family have a dog?   *Yes, the Carter family has a dog.*
10. Does Jessica have an English teacher? (no) *No, Jessica doesn't have an English teacher.*

PAGE 20   **ANSWERS TO THE WORKBOOK QUESTIONS**   **EXERCISE 2:**

1. *Her nationality is Tibetan. She's Tibetan.*   2. *It's Rita's jacket.*
3. *They're outside.*   4. *We're Canadian.*
5. *They're in class.*   6. *It's John's dog.*
7. *He's Margaret's son.*   8. *It's Mary's book.*
9. *He's from Canada.*

Teacher Guide

Teachers Guide ORAL QUESTIONS

How are you?

I'm fine, thank you.
I'm fine, thanks.
I'm so-so.
I'm not so good.
I'm not very well.

How are you doing?

I'm doing fine.
Just great!
I'm okay.

How are things going?

Things are going well.
Not badly.
Not so good.

To the teacher:
These greetings, found on page 22 of the Student Reader, are in common use.
Practice them at the beginning of each class,
as a way of greeting the students, so their response becomes automatic.

PAGE 21   **ANSWERS TO THE WORBOOK QUESTIONS**   **EXERCISE 1:**
1. Who does Harry meet?   Harry meets Jane.
2. Are they friends?   Yes, they're friends.
3. How is Jane?   Jane is fine.
4. How is Harry?   Things are not going well for Harry.
        Harry is not so good.
5. How are you?   I am _____.
6. How are you doing?   I'm doing fine.

PAGE 21   **ANSWERS TO THE WORKBOOK QUESTIONS**   **EXERCISE 2:**
1. Is Harry Jane's friend?   Yes, Harry is Jane's friend.
2. Is Jane sick?   No, Jane isn't sick.
        No, Jane is fine.
        Things are going well for Jane.
3. How is Harry?   Harry is not so good. Harry is sick
4. What does Jane ask Harry?   She asks, "How are you?"
5. How are you doing?   *Any suggested answers from page 21.*
6. Are you sick?   *Any suggested answers from page 21.*

LESSON 11 CONTINUED

PAGE 21   ANSWERS TO THE WORKBOOK QUESTIONS   EXERCISE 3:

1. I am fine, thank you.   How are you?
2. Things are going well at school.   How are things going at school?
3. I'm doing very well, thanks.   How are you doing?
4. I'm not so good.   How are you?
5. I'm okay.   How are you? or Are you okay?

PAGE 22   ANSWERS TO THE WORKBOOK QUESTIONS   EXERCISE 4:

sick	*not well*
bad	*not good*
at home	*where you live*
well	*fine*
week	*seven days*
notebook	*you write in it*
grandparents	*your mother or father's mother and father*
coffee	*you drink it*
pen	*you write with it*
How do you do?	*formal introduction*
negative	*no*
door	*where you walk into a room*

PAGE 22   ANSWERS TO THE WORKBOOK QUESTIONS   EXERCISE 5:

Harry is *sick* at home from school *today*. He *wants* to have some
mango *juice*. He goes to *town* where he meets Jane. She says, *Hi*
"Harry, *How* are you?" He says he's *not so good*. Jane
gives Harry her English *notebook*. He *says*, "Thanks Jane."

SEE NEXT PAGE.   ACTIVITY 7:
Copy page 50 of this guide, and cut the page into three cards. Divide the students into
groups of three and give each group one set of cards. The students are to find the answers
to the questions by asking each other the questions on their card. Encourage them to ask
the questions orally rather than just write the answers.

Review: Sylvia is a girl.
Walter is a boy.

GUIDE PAGE 50   ANSWERS TO THE GUIDE QUESTIONS   ACTIVITY 7:

Sylvia's middle name is Jane.   *Walter's middle name is John.*
Sylvia's first name is Sylvia.   *Walter's first name is Walter.*
Their surname is Johnson.
Their full names are Sylvia Jane Johnson and Walter John Johnson.

LESSON 11 CONTINUED
ACTIVITY 7:

SYLVIA _____ JOHNSON,   WALTER _____ JOHNSON

What is Sylvia's middle name?   _____

What is Walter's middle name?   _____

What is her first name?   _____

What is his first name?   _____

What is their surname?   _____

What are their full names?   _____

SYLVIA MARY _____   WALTER _____ _____

What is Sylvia's middle name?   _____

What is Walter's middle name?   _____

What is Sylvia's first name?   _____

What is Walter's first name?   _____

What is their surname?   _____

What are their full names?   _____

SYLVIA _____   WALTER JOHN _____

What is Sylvia's middle name?   _____

What is Walter's middle name?   _____

What is Sylvia's first name?   _____

What is Walter's first name?   _____

What is their surname?   _____

What are their full names?   _____

REVIEW

ORAL QUESTIONS

Are you Spanish?   *Yes, I'm Spanish.*
                                                   No, I'm not Spanish.

Does your mother come to English class?   *Yes, my mother comes to English class.*
                                                   No, my mother doesn't come to English class.

Does your mother live in Vietnam?   *Yes, my mother lives in Vietnam.*
                                                   No, my mother doesn't live in Vietnam.

Does your friend have a horse?   *Yes, my friend has a horse.*
                                                   No, my friend doesn't have a horse.

PAGE 25   ANSWERS TO THE STUDENT READER QUESTIONS   ACTIVITY 1:

1. Are they meeting?   *Yes, they are meeting.*
2. Are they shaking hands?   *No, they aren't shaking hands.*
3. Do you usually shake hands?   *Yes, I usually shake hands.*
                                                   No, I do not (don't) usually shake hands.
4. What do they say when they shake hands?   *They say, "How do you do?"*
5. Does she wear a dress?   No, she doesn't wear a dress.
6. Do they have shoes?   *Yes, they have shoes.*

7. **Is Toto a cat?**   *No, Toto isn't a cat.*
8. **Is your last name Carter?**   *No, my last name isn't Carter.*
9. **Do they have a dog?**   *Yes, they have a dog.*
10. **Does Ruth have a sister?**   *No, Ruth doesn't have a sister.*
11. **Does Craig have a son?**   *Yes, Craig has a son.*
12. **Does Ruth have a son?**   *No, Ruth doesn't have a son.*
13. **Are they a family?**   *Yes, they are a family.*
14. **Is Toto their dog?**   *Yes, Toto is their dog.*

15. **Does she have a T-shirt??**   *No, she doesn't have a T-shirt.*
16. **Does she talk to him?**   *No, she doesn't talk to him.*
17. **Does she wear a dress?**   *Yes, she wears a dress.*
18. **Does he have a hat?**   *No, he doesn't have a hat.*

PAGE 23   ANSWERS TO THE WORKBOOK QUESTIONS   EXERCISE 1:
Answer the questions in sentences:

1. Are they meeting?   *Yes, they are meeting.*
2. Are they shaking hands?   *Yes, they are shaking hands.*
3. Do you usually shake hands?   *Yes, I usually shake hands.*
                                                   No, I don't usually shake hands.
4. What do they say when they shake hands?   *They say, "How do you do?"*
5. Is it a formal introduction?   *Yes, it's a formal introduction.*
6. Do they have hats?   *No, they don't have hats.*

Teacher Guide   51

LESSON 12 CONTINUED

PAGE 23 ANSWERS TO THE WORKBOOK QUESTIONS CONTINUED EXERCISE 1:

7.	Is Toto a cat?	*No, Toto isn't a cat.*
8.	Is Carter their last name?	*Yes, Carter is their last name.*
9.	What is the dog's name?	*The dog's name is Toto.*
10.	Does Raymond have a father?	*Yes, Raymond has a father.*
11.	Does Craig have a wife?	*Yes, Craig has a wife.*
12.	Does Ruth have a husband?	*No, Ruth doesn't have a husband.*
13.	Are they a family?	*Yes, they are a family.*
14.	Is Toto their dog?	*Yes, Toto is their dog.*
15.	Do they have shoes?	*Yes, they have shoes.*
16.	Is Ruth French? (no)	*No, Ruth isn't French.*
17.	What is in his hand?	*He has his hat in his hand.*
18.	Does he have a jacket?	*Yes, he has a jacket.*

PAGE 24   ANSWERS TO THE WORKBOOK QUESTIONS   EXERCISE 2:

1. *Yes, they are friends.*
2. *Yes, the house has a door.*
3. *Yes, they are brothers.*
4. *No, they aren't from Paris.*
5. *No, he isn't a mother.*
6. *Yes, they are sisters. No, they aren't sisters.*
   No, they aren't brothers.
7. *No, it isn't my hat.*
8. *No, it isn't my friend's cup.*
9. *No, they aren't dogs.*
10. *No, she isn't my daughter.*
11. *Yes, I have a book.*
12. *No, it isn't my sister's jacket.*

PAGE 25   ANSWERS TO THE WORKBOOK QUESTIONS   EXERCISE 3:

1. *My dog is at home. I don't have a dog.*
2. *My surname is _____.*
3. *My mother 's name is _____.*
4. *I live in _____.(city)*
5. *I live in _____.(country)*
6. *Yes, the Carters have a dog.*
7. *Their dog's name is Toto.*
8. *Yes, Raymond Carter is a boy.*
9. *They are shoes.*

10. *Yes, Ruth has a brother.*
11. *Ruth's brother's name is Raymond.*
12. *No, Ruth is Jessica's daughter.*
13. *Yes, Jessica has a daughter.*
14. *My friend's name is _____.*
15. *I am from _____. (country)*
16. *Yes, I have a brother*
    No, I don't have a brother.
17. *Yes, my friends are American.*
    No, my friends aren't American.
18. *Yes, my mother lives in Portugal.*
    No, my mother doesn't live in Portugal.
19. *Yes, I have a sister.*
    No, I don't have a sister.
20. *I live in _____.(city)*

LESSON 12 CONTINUED

TEST 3 TOTAL MARKS: 50

ORAL QUESTIONS FOR TEST 3

QUESTIONS	ANSWERS
1. Does your father have a cat?	*Yes, my father has a cat. / No, my father doesn't have a cat.*
2. Do you have a husband?	*Yes, I have a husband. / No, I don't have a husband.*
3. What city are you from?	*I'm from _____.*
4. Do you meet your friends?	*Yes, I meet my friends. / No, I don't meet my friends.*
5. Are we in English class?	*Yes, we are in English class.*

ANSWERS FOR TEST 3
6. (10 marks)
Peter: Hello, I'm Peter.
Ruth: ***Hello, I'm Ruth.***
Peter: I'm pleased ***to meet you***.
Ruth: ***I'm pleased to meet*** you, too.

7 – 11 (4 marks each)
7. *Yes, my father has a hat. / No, my father doesn't have a hat.*
8. *Yes, the Carters have a dog.*
9. *No, Raymond isn't my brother.*
10. *Yes, I have a son. / No, I don't have a son.*
11. *Yes, we are (all) students.*

LESSONS 9 TO 12   TEST 3   NAME _____

Answer the questions in sentences. (4 marks each)

1. _____

2. _____

3. _____

4. _____

5. _____

---

6. **Peter and Ruth meet.** (10 marks)

Peter: Hello, I'm Peter.

Ruth: _____.

Peter: I'm pleased _____.

Ruth: _____ you, too.

Peter and Ruth

Answer the questions in sentences. (4 marks each)

7. Does your father have a hat?

_____

8. Do the Carters have a dog?

_____

9. Is Raymond your brother?

_____

10. Do you have a son?

_____

11. Are you all students?

_____

Teacher Guide

LESSON 13 Teachers Guide ORAL QUESTIONS

Do you have a watch?

Yes, I have a watch.
No, I don't have a watch.

Does he / she have a watch?

Yes, he / she has a watch.
No, he / she doesn't have a watch.

Does he / she have a necklace?

Yes, he / she has a necklace.
No, he / she doesn't have a necklace.

Does he / she have a glass?

Yes, he / she has a glass.
No, he / she doesn't have a glass.

Does he / she have a pen?

Yes, he / she has a pen
No, he / she doesn't have a pen.

Does he / she have a dress?

Yes, he / she has a dress.
No, he / she doesn't have a dress.

Does he / she have a ring?

Yes, he / she has a ring.
No, he / she doesn't have a ring.

Repeat the above questions. Use the following nouns until the students can answer fluently.
They may have difficulty with <u>don't</u> and <u>doesn't</u>.

match / box / wallet / pencil / toy / page

Does ___ (city) have a church?

Yes, _____ has a church.
No, _____ doesn't have a church.

Does ____ (city) have a bridge?

Yes, _____ has a bridge.
No, _____ doesn't have a bridge.

NOTE: The British say "hasn't got". This will be introduced later.

How many watches do you have?

I have _____ watches.
I have one watch.

How many watches does she / he have?

He / she has _____ watches.

Does he / she have _____ watches?

Yes, he / she has _____ watches.
No, he / she doesn't have ____ watches.

Continue asking questions as shown above using the following words.

necklaces / glasses / dishes / pens / dresses / books
matches / boxes / wallets / desks / pencils / toys / rings

NOTE: The first set of questions below is in the <u>plural</u> so <u>no article</u> is used.

Who has glasses?   _____ has glasses.
Who has matches?   _____ has matches.
Who has pens?   _____ has pens.

Continue using: pencils / rings / boxes
Note: This is difficult. It is introduced orally now and will be introduced formally later.
NOTE: This second set of questions is in the <u>singular</u> so an <u>article</u> is used.

Who has <u>a</u> necklace?   _____ has <u>a</u> necklace.
Who has <u>a</u> dress?   _____ has <u>a</u> dress.
Who has <u>a</u> wallet?   _____ has <u>a</u> wallet.

LESSON 13 CONTINUED

PAGE 26 **ANSWERS TO THE WORKBOOK QUESTIONS** **EXERCISE 1:**

bridge - *bridges*   watch - *watches*   face - *faces*   ring - *rings*
girl - *girls*   church - *churches*   wallet - *wallets*   page *pages*
dictionary - *dictionaries*   book - *books*   glass - *glasses*   toy - *toys*
desk - *desks*   pencil - *pencils*   box - *boxes*   match -*matches*
dish - *dishes*   dress - *dresses*   boy - *boys*   pen - *pens*

PAGE 26 **ANSWERS TO THE WORKBOOK QUESTIONS** **EXERCISE 2:**

1. How many books do you have?   *He / She has _____ book(s).*
2. How many watches do you have?   *He / She has _____ watch(es).*
3. How many faces do you have?   *He / She has one face.*
4. How many pens do you have?   *He / She has _____ pens.*
5. How many notebooks do you have?   *He / She has _____ notebooks.*
6. How many friends do you have?   *He / She has _____ friends.*

PAGE 26 **ANSWERS TO THE WORKBOOK QUESTIONS** **EXERCISE 3:**

watch   *necklace*   *ring*   *pencil*
book   *box*   *dish (plate)*   *toy*

PAGE 28 **ANSWERS TO THE STUDENT READER QUESTIONS**
ACTIVITY 3:

I have _____ ring(s).   *I have _____ wallet(s).*
I have _____ pencil(s).   *I have _____ book(s).*
I have _____ dictionary (ies).   *I have _____ match(es).*
I have _____ pen(s).   *I have _____ box(es).*
I have _____ toy(s).   *I have _____ dish(es).*

PAGE 28 **ANSWERS TO THE STUDENT BOOK QUESTIONS ACTIVITY 4:**

1. _____ has a watch.   *8. _____ has a ring.*
2. _____ has a wallet.   *9. A book has pages.*
3. _____ has a dictionary.   *10. _____ has glasses.*
4. There is / are _____ teacher(s) here.   *11. _____ has a box.*
5. _____ has a pencil.   *12. _____ has a box of matches.*
6. _____ has a book.   *13. _____ has a dish.*
7. _____ has a dress.   *14. _____ is a boy.*

PAGE 27 **ANSWERS TO THE WORKBOOK QUESTIONS** **EXERCISE 4:**

NARRATOR: Carol and Tom are talking about their English *class* in *Canada*.
CAROL: This is a very *nice* room.
TOM: We have *so many* good things. We have comfortable *desks*,
interesting *books* and a good board for our teacher to *write* on.
CAROL: I like all the students. We laugh and talk about our *mistakes*.
I like to look out the *window* the mountains.
TOM: I like English classes. I study at *home*.
CAROL: So do I!

LESSON 13 CONTINUED

PAGE 27   **ANSWERS TO THE WORKBOOK QUESTIONS**   **EXERCISE 5:**

classroom	*a school room*
shake hands	*you do it when you are introduced*
comfortable	*nice to sit on*
interesting	*you want to know more*
notebook	*you write in it*
partner	*a friend you work with*
numbers	*one, two, three...*
desks	*you sit at them to write*
home	*where you live*

PAGE 26   **STUDENT READER**   **ACTIVITY 5:**
FIND A PARTNER

To the teacher:

One student is to read a singular noun from page 26, (Student Reader),
the second is to say the plural.
Then the second student is to choose a singular noun and the first is to say the plural.
Continue in this manner until all the words on page 26 have been reviewed.

EXAMPLE: First person - "page"   Second person -"pages"

PAGE 58 GUIDE   **ACTIVITY 6**

NOTE: Use this activity if the students need more practice with these nouns.
Photocopy the pictures on Page 26 of the Student Reader and the noun cards below.
Make one complete set for each group of two or three students.
Each group of students is to deal out their set of picture cards.
Each group is to put one set of the noun cards below, face down.

The first student is to pick up a noun card and ask any other group member:
Do you have a _____?

If the student asked, has a _____ then they give it to the one who asked the question.

OR

The cards may be dealt out as above and the students will ask:
What is in box number _____.
The student with the card answers,
There is a _____ in box number _____.
There are _____ in box number _____.

LESSON 13 CONTINUED

ACTIVITY 7:

a church	a watch	mountains
a necklace	a glass	motorcycle
a dish	a pen	a face
a dress	chair	a ring
a bridge	a match	a box
a wallet	a desk	a pencil
a toy	a page	a window

LESSON 14 Teachers Guide ORAL QUESTIONS

Does a man have a dress?   *No, a man doesn't have a dress.*

Does _____ live in Delhi?   *No, _____ doesn't live in Delhi.*

Continue using: **Paris / London / Hong Kong**

Do you have a toy?   *Yes, I have a toy.*

       No, I don't have a toy.

To the teacher: Now go to another student and ask this next question as you point to the student you just asked.

Does she / he have a toy?   *Yes, she / he has a toy.*

       No, she / he doesn't have a toy.

Continue using: **house / hat / cat**

The British form, using <u>have got</u>, <u>haven't got</u>, is introduced in the next book.

Are you British?   *Yes, I'm British.*

       No, I'm not British.

Are they French?   *Yes, they're French.*

       No, they're not French.

Are you two Spanish?   *Yes, we're Spanish.*

       No, we're not Spanish.

Continue using: **American / Canadian / French / German / Chinese/ Japanese**

Do you have a daughter?   *Yes, I have a daughter.*

       No, I don't have a daughter.

Does she have a daughter?   *Yes, she has a daughter.*

       No, she doesn't have a daughter.

Continue using: son / father / mother / sister / brother / grandmother / grandfather

USING "SOME" AND "ANY"

Do you have some hamburgers?   *Yes, I have some hamburgers.*

       No, I don't have any hamburgers.

Do I have some pencils?   *Yes, you have some pencils.*

       No, you don't have any pencils.

Does she have some mango juice?   *Yes, she has some mango juice.*

       No, she doesn't have any mango...

Do they have some jackets?   *Yes, they have some jackets.*

       No, they don't have any jackets.

Does he have some pencils?   *Yes, he has some pencils.*

       No, he doesn't have any pencils.

Do we have some birds?   *Yes, we have some birds.*

       No, we don't have any birds.

LESSON 14 CONTINUED

PAGE 28   **ANSWERS TO THE WORKBOOK QUESTIONS:**   **EXERCISE 1:**

1. *Yes, I have a wallet.*   *No, I don't have a wallet.*
2. *Yes, I have a desk.*   *No, I don't have a desk.*
3. *Yes, my mother has a ring.*   *No, my mother doesn't have a ring.*
4. *Yes, I have a face.*
5. *Yes, I have a necklace.*   *No, I don't have a necklace.*
6. *Yes, I have a father in Canada.*   *No, I don't have a father in Canada.*
7. *Yes, I have an American sister.*   *No, I don't have an American sister.*

PAGE 28   **ANSWERS TO THE WORKBOOK QUESTIONS**   **EXERCISE 2:**

1. I She doesn't have any coffee.   *Does she have some coffee?*
2. I don't have any juice.   *Do you have some juice? (any juice)*
3. They have some cars.   *Do they have some cars?*

PAGE 28   **ANSWERS TO THE WORKBOOK QUESTIONS:**   **ACTIVITY 1:**

1. Do you have some dogs?   *Yes, he/she has some dogs.*
                                           No, he/she doesn't have any dogs.

2. Does _____(name) have some necklaces?   *Yes, ____ has some necklaces.*
                                           No, _____ doesn't have any necklaces.

3. Do you have some rings?   *Yes, he/she has some rings.*
                                           No, he/she doesn't have any rings.

4. Do you have some matches?   *Yes, he/she has some matches.*
                                           No, he/she doesn't have any matches.

5. Are there some pages in your book?   *Yes, there are some pages in his/her book.*
                                           No, there aren't any pages in his/her book.

6. Does your friend have some cats?   *Yes, his/her friend has some cats.*
                                           No, his/her friend doesn't have any cats.

PAGE 30   **ANSWERS TO THE WORKBOOK QUESTIONS:**   **EXERCISE 3:**
Look at the pictures and answer these questions in sentences.

1. Do you see some mountains?   *Yes, I see <u>some</u> mountains.*
2. Do you see some motorcycles?   *No, I don't see <u>any</u> motorcycles.*
3. Do they have some chairs?   *Yes, they have <u>some</u> chairs.*
4. Do you see some bridges?   *No, I don't see <u>any</u> bridges.*
5. Do the students have some desks?   *Yes, the students have <u>some</u> desks.*

LESSON 14 CONTINUED

ACTIVITY 3:   REVIEW
Minimum – 4 students. Divide into groups of not more than 6 students.
Photocopy this page and cut it into six cards. Give each student one card.
They are to get the missing information about Penny. To do this, they must ask:
What is her name?   What is her address?   What city is she from?
What country is she from?   What is her nationality?

PENNY   PENNY

FULL NAME: PENNY WILSON   FULL NAME: _____

ADDRESS: _____   ADDRESS: 123 Vancouver Street

CITY:_____ COUNTRY:_____   CITY:_____ COUNTRY:_____

NATIONALITY: _____   NATIONALITY: _____

*********************************   *************************************

PENNY   PENNY

FULL NAME: _____   FULL NAME: _____

ADDRESS: _____   ADDRESS: _____

CITY: Victoria COUNTRY:_____   CITY:_____ COUNTRY:_____

NATIONALITY: _____   NATIONALITY: Canadian

*********************************   *************************************

PENNY   PENNY

FULL NAME: _____   FULL NAME: _____

ADDRESS: _____   ADDRESS: _____

CITY:_____ COUNTRY: Canada   CITY:_____ COUNTRY:_____

NATIONALITY: _____   NATIONALITY: _____

LESSON 14 CONTINUED

ACTIVITY 4:   REVIEW
This is the same as Activity 3, but it is about Norman.
The two activities may be done at the same time or separately.

NORMAN

    FULL NAME: _____

    ADDRESS: _____

    CITY:_____ COUNTRY:_____

    NATIONALITY: _____

NORMAN

FULL NAME: NORMAN WALL

ADDRESS: 567 Princess Street

CITY:_____ COUNTRY:_____

NATIONALITY: _____

*********************************** ***************************************

NORMAN

FULL NAME: _____

ADDRESS: _____

CITY:_____ COUNTRY: Canada

NATIONALITY: _____

NORMAN

FULL NAME: _____

ADDRESS: _____

CITY:_____ COUNTRY:_____

NATIONALITY: Canadian

*********************************** ***************************************

NORMAN

FULL NAME: _____

ADDRESS: _____

CITY: Victoria COUNTRY:_____

NATIONALITY: _____

NORMAN

FULL NAME: _____

ADDRESS: _____

CITY:_____ COUNTRY:_____

NATIONALITY: _____

*********************************** ***************************************

LESSON 15 Teachers Guide

ORAL QUESTIONS

Do you like the theater?

Yes, I like the theater.
No, I don't like the theater.

Do you like this city?

Yes, I like this city.
No, I don't like this city.

Do you like your town?

Yes, I like my town.
No, I don't like my town.

Does she like her town?

Yes, she likes her town.
No, she doesn't like her town.

Do you go to the theater?

Yes, I go to the theater.
No, I don't go to the theater.

Is this a big table?

Yes, this (it) is a big table.
No, this (it) isn't a big table.

Do you speak Russian?

Yes, I speak Russian.
No, I don't speak Russian.

Do you speak French?

Yes, I speak French.
No, I don't speak French.

Answer using object pronouns.
Do you see the door?
Do you see your friend?

Yes, I see it.
Yes, I see him / her.
No, I can't see him / her.

Can you see Mary and John?

Yes, I can see them.
No, I can't see them.

Do you read books?

Yes, I read them.
No, I don't read them.

Do you live in India?

Yes, I live in India.
No, I don't live in India.

Does he live in India? (Point to the student who answered.)

Yes, he lives in India.
No, he doesn't live in India.

Continue using: Canada / The Czech Republic / The United States / China / India / France / Mexico / Nepal / England / Vietnam / Tibet

To the teacher:
Tell the students to use a / an when the listener doesn't know which thing you mean.
Review that "one" can be used as a pronoun.

Do you have an apple?

Yes, I have an apple.
Yes, I have one.
No, I don't have an apple.
No, I don't have one.

LESSON 15 CONTINUED

PAGE 31   **ANSWERS TO THE WORKBOOK QUESTIONS**   **EXERCISE 1:**

1.   Yes, I see her. No, I don't see her.
2.   Yes, I see it.   No, I don't see it.
3.   Yes, I see him. No, I don't see him.
4.   Yes, I see them.   No, I don't see them.
5.   Yes, I have it. No, I don't have it.
6.   Yes, I have them.   No, I don't have them.
7.   Yes, I have it. No, I don't have it.
8.   Yes, I have it. No, I don't have it.
9.   Yes, I see them.   No, I don't see them.
10.   Yes, I see him. No, I don't see him.

PAGE 31   **ANSWERS TO THE WORKBOOK QUESTIONS**   **EXERCISE 2:**

1. They have <u>a</u> cat.   6.   There is <u>an</u> apple.
2. <u>The</u> man's name is John.   7.   <u>The</u> first lesson is here.
3. There is <u>a</u> OR <u>the</u> church. 8.   There is <u>a</u> OR <u>the</u> toy.
4. <u>The</u> dog Toto is here.   9.   She has <u>a</u> OR <u>the</u> desk.
5. He sees <u>a</u> car.   10.   They go to <u>the</u> small theater.

NOTE: Use "the" if it is understood which "church", "toy" or "desk".
Use "THE" if it is SPECIFIC.

PAGE 32   **ANSWERS TO THE WORKBOOK QUESTIONS**   **EXERCISE 3:**

*1. Do you have <u>**a**</u> friend?   Yes, I have <u>**a**</u> friend.*
*2. Who is <u>**the**</u> teacher?   <u>**The**</u> teacher is _____.*
*3. Can I have <u>**a**</u> pen?   Yes, you can have <u>**a**</u> pen.*
*4. Where is <u>**an**</u> apple?   Here is <u>**an**</u> apple.*
*5. Does she have <u>**a**</u> son?   No, she doesn't have <u>**a**</u> son.*
*6. Do some people have <u>**a**</u> middle name?   Yes, some people have <u>**a**</u> middle name.*
*7. Where is <u>**the**</u> red English book?   <u>**The**</u> red English book is here.*
*8. Do you go to <u>**the**</u> big theater?   Yes, I go to <u>**the**</u> big theater.*
*9. Do you see <u>**a**</u> cat? No, I don't see <u>**a**</u> cat.*
*10. What is <u>**the**</u> verb in this sentence? <u>**The**</u> verb is "is".*

PAGE 32   **ANSWERS TO THE WORKBOOK QUESTIONS**   **EXERCISE 4:**

1.   Yes, I have <u>it</u>. No, I don't have <u>it</u>.
2.   Yes, I meet <u>them</u>.   No, I don't meet <u>them</u>.
3.   Yes, I do <u>it</u>.   No, I don't do <u>it</u>.
4.   Yes, I see <u>him</u>. No, I don't see <u>him</u>.
5.   Yes, I see <u>them</u>.   No, I don't see <u>them</u>.
6.   Yes, I like <u>her.</u> No, I don't like <u>her.</u>
7.   Yes, I see <u>them</u>.   No, I don't see <u>them</u>.
8.   Yes, I see <u>one</u>. OR, I see <u>it</u>.   No, I don't see <u>it</u> / <u>one</u>.

LESSON 16 Teachers Guide

ORAL QUESTIONS REVIEW (Lessons 13 to 16)
Note: The students need to review the oral questions often.

What is your surname?	*My surname is _____*
Is this your pen?	*Yes, it is my pen. No, it isn't my pen.*
Is she your friend?	*Yes, she is my friend.*
Is your dog outside sometimes?	*Yes, my dog is outside sometimes.*
Is this your shoe?	*Yes, it is my shoe. No, it's not my shoe.*
	No, it isn't my shoe.
Is this his pen?	*Yes, it is his pen. No, it isn't his pen.*
Do you have a daughter?	*Yes, I have a daughter.*
	No, I don't have a daughter.
Do you have a tie?	*Yes, I have a tie. No, I don't have a tie.*
Do you have a son in Nepal?	*Yes, I have a son in Nepal.*
	No, I don't have a son in Nepal.
What country are you from?	*I am from _____.*
Do you have a wife?	*Yes, I have a wife.*
	No, I don't have a wife.
Does he have a watch?	*Yes, he has a watch.*
	No, he doesn't have a watch.
Do you live in Canada?	*No, I don't live in Canada.*
Is there one student here?	*Yes, there is one student here.*
	No, there are _____ students here.
Do you have one ring?	*Yes, I have one ring.*
	No, I have _____ rings.

Continue using – ring, dress, watch, necklace, wallet

Are you from France?	*Yes, I'm from France.*
	No, I'm not from France.
	No, I'm from _____.
Can you speak Spanish?	*Yes, I can speak Spanish.*
	No, I can't speak Spanish.

OBJECT PRONOUNS

Can you see a big dog?	*Yes, I can see <u>it</u>.*
	No, I can't see <u>it</u>.
Can you see your mother?	*Yes, I can see <u>her</u>.*
	No, I can't see <u>her</u>.
Do you see your friends?	*Yes, I see <u>them</u>.*
	No, I don't see <u>them</u>.
Do they see you and me?	*Yes, they see <u>us</u>.*
Can we see the students?	*Yes, we can see <u>them</u>.*

LESSON 16 CONTINUED

ORAL QUESTIONS CONTINUED
SOME / ANY

Do you have some glasses?

Yes, I have some glasses.
No, I don't have any glasses.

Do you see some flowers?

Yes, I see some flowers.
No, I don't see any flowers.

Do you have some boats?

Yes, I have some boats.
No, I don't have any boats.

Do you see some birds?

Yes, I see some birds.
No, I don't see any birds.

Do you have some brushes?

Yes, I have some brushes.
No, I don't have any brushes.

PAGE 33   ANSWERS TO THE WORKBOOK QUESTIONS   EXERCISE 1:

1. watches
2. brushes
3. dresses
4. glasses
5. faces
6. churches
7. pens
8. rings
9. wallets
10. necklaces
11. desks
12. dictionaries

PAGE 33   ANSWERS TO THE WORKBOOK QUESTIONS   ACTIVITY 2:

1. There are _____ students in this class.
2. He/She has _____ pens.
   He/She doesn't have any pens.
3. He/She wears glasses.
   He/She doesn't wear glasses.
4. There are three birds in Activity 1.
5. There are _____ boys in this class.
6. There are _____ pencils on this desk.
7. There are ____ pages in this book.
8. There are _____ churches in this city.
9. No, his/her dog doesn't speak English.
10. No, his/her cat doesn't read.
11. Yes, his/her book has twenty pages.
    No, his/her book doesn't have twenty pages.

PAGE 34   ANSWERS TO THE WORKBOOK QUESTIONS   EXERCISE 2:

1. Yes, I see _them_. No, I don't see _them_.
2. Yes, I have _it_. No, I don't have _it_.
3. Yes, I read _them_. No, I don't read _them_.
4. No, I don't see _her_.
5. No, the man doesn't have _it_.
6. No, I can't meet _them_.
7. No, we don't see _them_.
8. No, I don't see _him_.

PAGE 34   ANSWERS TO THE WORKBOOK QUESTIONS   EXERCISE 3:

1. No, he doesn't have a tie.
2. No, this isn't London.
3. No, I'm not a mother.
4. No, she doesn't have a hat.
5. No, she doesn't drink Sprite.
6. No, I'm not a grandfather.
7. No, they aren't outside.
8. No, they're not Canadians.

LESSON 16 CONTINUED

ACTIVITY 3:   **REVIEW**
Put these examples on the blackboard.
Make <u>one copy</u> of the chart below and give <u>one name to each student.</u>
The students are to introduce themselves to their friends, using a name from below.
Then they are tell them how they are. (The use of "good" is an idiom here.)

EXAMPLE: **PAUL:** *Hi! I'm Paul. How are you?*   **KATE:** *Hi, I'm Kate. I'm not so good.*

MARGARET I'm fine.	JOHN Very well, thanks.	SUSAN I'm so-so.	NANCY Just great!
CAROL Not so good.	DANIEL I'm not very well.	BRUCE I'm doing fine.	HELEN I'm okay.
RITA Not badly.	PETER I'm fine.	PAUL I am fine, thanks.	DAVID I'm not so good.
MARIA I'm so-so.	HOLLY Not badly.	ROBERT I'm okay.	MARK Very well, thanks.

ANSWERS FOR TEST 4

Questions 1 - 25   (2 marks each)

1. one   *face*
2. two   *box*
3. three   *dish plate*
4. four   *pen*
5. five   *match*
6. six   *wallet*
7. seven   *toy*
8. eight   *book*
9. nine   *necklace*
10. ten   *ring*
11. eleven   *pencil*
12. twelve   *bridge*

PLURALS:

13. girl *girls*
14. dictionary *dictionaries*
15. match *matches*
16. boy *boys*
17. pencil *pencils*
18. glass *glasses*

19. The Carters don't have *a* cat.

20. In the Carter family, Craig is *the* father.

21. He sees Mary and Jim. Do you see *them*?

22. Here she comes. Do you see *her*?

23. We are here. Do you see *us*?

24. There is a dog. Do you see *it*?

25. Any suggested answers from page 21 of the Student Reader.

Teacher Guide   67

LESSONS 13 TO 16   TEST 4

NAME _____

Write the number and name in each box.
(questions 1 to 25 – 2 marks each)

1 _____	2 _____	3 _____	4 _____
5 _____	6 _____	7 _____	8 _____
9 _____	10 _____	11 _____	12 _____

Write the plural for each word.

13. girl _____   14. dictionary _____   15.match _____

16. boy _____   17. pencil _____   18. glass _____

Use <u>a</u> or <u>the</u> in the sentences:

19. The Carters don't have _____ cat.   20. In the Carter family, Craig is ____ father.

Use an object pronoun in the sentences:

21. He sees Mary and John. Do you see _____?   22. Here she comes. Do you see _____?

23. We are here. Do you see _____? 24. There is a dog. Do you see _____?

Answer this question in a sentence:

25. How are you? _____.

Teacher Guide

LESSON 17 - Teachers Guide

ORAL QUESTIONS

ASK THESE QUESTIONS MANY TIMES.

What is behind her?   *There is a _____ behind her.*
What is behind you?   *There is a _____ behind me.*
Who is in front of you?   *_____ is in front of me.*
Who is behind you?   *_____ is behind me.*
Where is the door?   *The door is beside / behind them.*
Where are the windows?   *The windows are _____ her / him / them.*
Who is beside you?   *_____ is beside me.*
Who is between _____ and _____?   *_____ is between us / them.*
Where am I?   *I am in front of you.*

A REVIEW OF PREPOSITIONS

What is on your desk?   *My _____ is on my desk.*
Where is your pencil?   *My pencil is in my hand / on my desk.*
What is in my hand?   *There is a pen in your hand.*

Where is your book?   *My book is on the (my) desk.*
Where is the picture?   *The picture is on the wall.*
Where are the curtains?   *The curtains are at the windows.*

Where is my pen?   *Your pen is in your hand.*
Where are you?   *I am in an English class.*
What is in your pocket?   *There is a _____ in my pocket.*

Note to the teacher: Point to some objects in the room and ask questions like those above.

The students should use these prepositions:
on,   in,   at,   between,   beside,   under,   behind, in front of

PAGE 35   **ANSWERS TO THE WORKBOOK QUESTIONS.**   **EXERCISE 1:**
Use these prepositions to complete the sentences.
on   behind   in   under   beside   between   in front of

1. *The lady is <u>on</u> the elephant.*
2. *The man is <u>under</u> the car.*
3. *The dog is <u>behind</u> the lady.*
4. *The cat is <u>on</u> the house.*
5. *The elephant and the car are <u>in front of</u> the house.*
6. *The man is <u>beside / under</u> the tree.*
7. *The door is <u>between</u> the windows.*
8. *The tree is <u>beside / in front of</u> the house.*

LESSON 17 CONTINUED

PAGE 35   **ANSWERS TO THE WORKBOOK QUESTIONS**   **EXERCISE 2:**

1. Where is the tree? — *The tree is beside/ in front of the house.*
2. Where is the elephant? — *The elephant is in front of the house.*
3. Where is the dog? — *The dog is behind the lady.*
4. Where is the door? — *The door is between the windows.*
5. Where is the man? — *The man is under the car / tree.*

PAGE 36   **ANSWERS TO THE WORKBOOK QUESTIONS**   **EXERCISE 3:**

1. *My dog isn't in front of me. / My dog is not in front of me.*
2. *He / She is in front of / behind / beside me.*
3. *They are on my desk.*
4. *My chair is under me.*
5. *No, my cat isn't with me.*
6. *He / She is with me. / He / She is in his / her classroom.*
7. *_____ (name) is behind me. / The _____ (window) is behind me.*
8. *It is on my desk.*
9. *There are books on it. / There is a pen on it.*
10. *Yes, they are on the wall.*

PAGE 36   **ANSWERS TO THE WORKBOOK QUESTIONS**   **EXERCISE 4:**

1. Our cat is *the* big one. — Do you see *it*?
2. Here is *a* good book. — It is for *him* / *her* / *you*.
3. They are *our* / *the* English teachers. — Do you like *them*?
4. We are *the* students. — Do you see *us*?
5. Here is *a* / *my* / *our* teacher.
6. They are my dogs. — Do you like *them*?
7. The gray one is gentle. — Do you want *it*?
8. This is *a* toy. — You can have *it*.

PAGE 35   **ANSWERS TO THE STUDENT READER QUESTIONS**   **ACTIVITY 1:**

1. Where do they sit? — *They sit at a table.*
2. Where is the teacup? — *The teacup is on the table.*
3. Where is the window? — *The window is behind them.*
4. Where is their work? — *Their work is on the table.*
5. What is the iron? — *The iron is between them.*

6. What does she do? — *She eats.*
7. Where does she sit? — *She sits at a table.*
8. Where are the people? — *The people are behind her.*
9. Where is the table? — *The table is in front of her.*

10. What do they sit on? — *They sit on chairs.*
11. Do they have some books? — *Yes, they have some books.*
12. Where are their shoes? — *Their shoes are on the floor.*
13. Do they read? — *Yes, they read.*

LESSON 18 Teachers Guide

Note to the teacher: In North America and Australia, the ground floor of a building is 1.
In Europe, the ground floor is 0 and the next floor up is 1.

ORAL QUESTIONS

What street do you live on?	*I live on _____. (Queen Street.)*
What city do you live in?	*I live in _____. (city name)*
Where do you live? (with number)	*I live at _____ (42 Queen Street)*
Where do you live? (without number)	*I live on _____. (Queen Street))*
Do you have a neighbor?	*Yes, I have a neighbor.*
Is she / he your neighbor?	*Yes, she / he is my neighbor.*
	No, she / he isn't my neighbor.
What is your neighbor's address?	*His/Her address is ___. (44 Queen St.)*
Do you live beside him/her? (indicate another student)	*Yes, I live beside him/her.*

PAGE 37   **ANSWERS TO THE WORKBOOK QUESTIONS**   **EXERCISE 1:**

1. *Yes, Raymond Carter is an Australian.*
2. *Ming lives in Australia.*
3. *Ming's parents come from China.*
4. *Raymond Carter's address is 11 Kent Street.*
5. *Nancy lives on the third floor of the apartment building.*
6. *Yes, Ming is Chinese Australian.*
7. *Raymond's sister's name is Ruth.*
   Her name is Ruth.
8. *Ming's address is 13 Kent Street.*
9. *Ruth's friend is Nancy.*
10. *Ming and Nancy are Raymond and Ruth's neighbors.*
    Ming and Nancy are their neighbors.
11. *They all live on Kent Street.*
12. *I live on _____.*

PAGE 38   **ANSWERS TO THE WORKBOOK QUESTIONS**   **EXERCISE 2:**

neighbor	*someone who lives beside you*
apartment	*many people have homes in one building*
classroom	*the room where you learn from your teacher*

PAGE 38   **ANSWERS TO THE WORKBOOK QUESTIONS**   **ACTIVITY 2:**
FIRST STUDENT:

Where do you live? (street)	*He / she lives on _____.*
Where do you live? (street and number)	He / She lives at _____.
City:	*He / She lives in _____.*
What is your address? (example)	*11 Kent Street, Victoria, B.C. Canada (postal code)*

LESSON 18 CONTINUED

ACTIVITY 4:

INSTRUCTIONS: **WHO LIVES ON YOUR STREET?**

There are two sets of role cards for this activity - 1 to 7, and 8 to 15.

Number 15 is to be used if there is an uneven number of students present.

Distribute the role cards 1 to 7 on one side of the room, and 8 to 15 on the other side so that one student from each side lives on each street.

EXAMPLE: Number 1 and 8, Number 2 and 9. Each student is given <u>one role-card</u>.

STUDENT NAMES: New English names are used here. Explain which are male and female.

Tell the students to use the pronouns <u>he/she</u> or <u>his/her</u> or <u>my</u> to answer the questions.

Put the following questions on the blackboard.

What is your name?   *His / Her name is _____.*

What street do you live on?   *He / She lives on _____.*

Who lives on your street?   _____ *lives on my street.*

Where does he / she live on your street?   *He / She lives at (number and street).*

NOTE: **When the students have completed Activity 4, the teacher should ask:**
Where do you live on your street? What street do you live on?

ROLE CARDS:

1. **SUSAN** 14 Kingsway Road	2. **CAMILLE / CAMERON** 27 Imperial Street	3. **KATE** 49 Royal Road
4. **MARIA** 88 Grandview Road	5. **ALLAN** 96 Fraser Street	6. **NOREEN / NICK** 45 Edward Road
7. **BRUCE** 72 Winston Road		

8. **MARGARET** 82 Kingsway Road	9. **RUTH / JOSEPH** 94 Imperial Street	10. **RICHARD / MARION** 15 Royal Road
11. **EDWARD** 29 Grandview Road	12. **DANIEL** 33 Fraser Street	13. **JUSTIN** 75 Edward Road
14. **JACK** 38 Winston Road		15. **OLGA** 69 Kingsway Road

LESSON 18 CONTINUED

This game may not be suitable for all groups.

ACTIVITY 5:   DRAW-IT GAME   DIRECTIONS
The class is divided into four groups. The teacher takes one person from the first group into the hall, and gives them the name of a noun. Once the person has heard the noun, they have two minutes to draw it on the board, and their group must name the noun before the two minutes are up.

If they can name the noun by looking at the drawing within two minutes, they get 5 points. If they cannot guess what it is within the two minutes, they don't get any points.

Each group has a turn, sending one person out to hear the word, and then trying to guess the word from the drawing before the time is up. The team with the most points wins the game.

LIST OF NOUNS

dog	student	curtains	shoe	man
bird	jacket	tie	apple	lady
hat	door	house	family	clock
cat	pen	table	church	picture
watch	boy	necklace	glass	window

WORKBOOK PAGE 39   BINGO   ACTIVITY 3:
Have the students print all of the words in the WORDS TO PRINT list into any of the empty BINGO squares. Each student should place the words randomly so that all of the printed cards are different.

Give each student a number of small objects such as beans or stones to place over the boxes as the words are called.

The teacher or a student then calls the words in the WORDS TO CALL list, allowing the students time to find the matching word. Some help is given as the game is played, as the goal is for the students to learn the vocabulary.

The winner(s) of the game call BINGO when they have a straight and complete row of covered boxes. The covered rows can be in a straight vertical line, a straight horizontal line, or a straight diagonal line. The diagonal line must go from one corner to the other.

The FREE box is counted as a covered word when it is a part of the completed row.

The game can be played a number of times until the students know the vocabulary well.

LESSON 19 ORAL QUESTIONS

NOTE: **The teacher uses his / her hand to indicate the place.**

Who is the third / sixth student here/there?   _____ *is the third /sixth student here / there.*
Continue asking using the ordinal numbers introduced on Page.

How many people are in your family?   *There are __ people in my family.*
How many teachers are here?   *There is one teacher here.*
How many students are here?   *There are _____ students here.*
                              Possessive pronouns
Is this book yours?   *Yes, it's mine. / No, it isn't mine.*
Is this his / hers?   *Yes, it's his/hers. No, it isn't his/hers.*
Are these desks theirs?   *Yes, they're theirs. / No, they aren't theirs.*
Whose is this _____?   *It's his. / It's hers.*

Place different things in front of the students and ask: Is this his / hers / theirs?

| PAGE 40 | ANSWERS TO THE WORKBOOK QUESTIONS | EXERCISE 1: |

1. *Yes, it's mine.*
2. *This is ours. / It's ours.*
3. *It's hers.*
4. *Yes, it's theirs. / No, it isn't theirs.*
5. *It's mine.*
6. *Yes, it's ours. / No, it isn't ours.*
7. *Yes, it's his. / No, it isn't his.*
8. *Yes, they're theirs. / No, they aren't theirs.*

| PAGE 37 | ANSWERS TO THE STUDENT READER QUESTIONS | ACTIVITY 1: |

1. My pens are on my desk.
2. *My desk is beside my chair.*
3. *The desks are between the window and me.*
4. _____ *is in front of me.*
5. *My books / pens are on my desk.*

6. *My desk is under my book.*
7. *My books are in my desk.*
8. *A student is at the door.*
9. *A desk is beside me.*
10. *The students are behind me.*

LESSON 19 CONTINUED

PAGE 40   **ANSWERS TO THE WORKBOOK QUESTIONS**   **EXERCISE 2:**

1.   There are _____ students here.
2.   There are _____ books on the desk.
3.   There are _____ desks here.
4.   There is/are _____ teacher(s) here.
5.   There are _____ pens on my desk.

PAGE 40   **ANSWERS TO THE WORKBOOK QUESTIONS**   **EXERCISE 3:**

1.   Where is your pen?   *My pen is / on my desk / in my hand.*
2.   Where is your book?   *My book is / on my desk / in my desk.*
3.   Who is behind you?   _____ *(name) is behind me.*
4.   What is in front of you?   *The teacher's desk is in front of me.*
5.   What is under your book?   *My desk is under my book.*
6.   Who is beside you?   _____ *is beside me.*

PAGE 41   ANSWERS TO THE WORKBOOK QUESTIONS   EXERCISE 4:

1. I live **_in_** a house.
2. I get up **_at_** six o'clock.
3. I si*t **_at_*** my desk.

9. No one is **_on_** the bridge.
10. The water is **_under_** the bridge.
11. The teacher is **_in front of, behind_** / **_beside_** me.

4. I live **_in_** _____(city name).
5.   I go to school / work **_with_** my friend.
6. We live **_beside_** our neighbors.
7. They are **_in_** the city.
8. I sit **_in front of, beside, behind_** my friend.

12. The toy is **_in_** / **_on_** the box.
13. The door is **_beside_** / **_behind_** / **_in front of_** me.
14. I study English **_with_** my friends.
15. She lives **_in_** an apartment.
16. She lives **_on_** the third floor

LESSON 20   REVIEW

ORAL QUESTIONS

To the teacher: We suggest that you do a review of any of the Oral Questions that the **students** have found difficult.

For the following Oral Questions, as you move about the room, pick up an item belonging to a student and ask them if it's theirs, while indicating another student with your hand. In this way, you can review the possessive pronouns.

Is this your pen?   *Yes, it's mine.*
                           No, it isn't mine.

Is this his book?   *Yes, it's his.*
                           No, it isn't his.

Is this her red pen?   *Yes, it's hers.*
                           No, it isn't hers.

Is this your green T-shirt? *Yes, it's mine.*
                           No, it isn't mine.

Is this our classroom?   *Yes, it's ours.*

PAGE 42   ANSWERS TO THE WORKBOOK QUESTIONS   EXERCISE 1:

1. Do you have your <u>books</u>?   *Yes, I have **them**.*
2. Do you see the <u>teacher</u>?   *Yes, I see **him** / **her**.*
3. Does this city have <u>churches</u>?   *Yes, it has <u>them</u> / **some**.*
4. Do you see the <u>dog</u>?   *Yes, I see **it**.*
5. Do you meet your <u>friends</u>?   *Yes, I meet **them**. No, I don't meet **them**.*
6. Do you see your friends?   *Yes, I see **them**. No, I don't see **them**.*
7. Do you see Mary's <u>house</u>?   *Yes, I see **it**. No, I don't see **it**.*
8. Do you speak <u>German</u>?   *Yes, I speak <u>it</u>. No, I don't speak **it**.*

PAGE 42   ANSWERS TO THE WORKBOOK QUESTIONS   EXERCISE 2:

1. Where is your pen?   *My pen is **on** my desk. / in my hand.*
2. Who is at the door?   _____ *is **at** the door.*
3. Who is beside you?   _____ *is <u>beside</u> me.*
4. **Who is between ____ and ____?**   _____ *is **between** ____ and ____ .*
5. **What is in front of you?**   _____ *is **in front of** me.*
6. **What is under your desk?**   _____ *is **under my desk**.*

PAGE 42   ANSWERS TO THE WORKBOOK QUESTIONS   EXERCISE 3:

1. This is my book. Whose book is it?   *It's mine.*
2. The students have pens. Whose pens are they   *They're theirs.*
3. Whose classroom is this?   *It's ours.*
4. The boy has a toy. Whose toy is it?   *It's his.*

LESSON 20 CONTINUED

MID TERM TEST 5 TOTAL MARKS: 100

ORAL QUESTIONS FOR THE MID TERM TEST 5

QUESTIONS	ANSWERS
1. How are you?	Any suggested answers from page 21.
2. Does your mother have a daughter?	*Yes, my mother has a daughter.*
	No, she doesn't have a daughter.
3. How many students are here?	*There are _____ students here.*
4. What city are you from?	*I'm from _____.*
5. Does your friend go to Mexico?	*Yes, my friend goes to Mexico.*
	No, my friend doesn't go to Mexico.
6. You have a pen. Whose pen is it?	*It's mine. / It's my pen.*
7. Are your friends Canadian?	*Yes, my friends are Canadian.*
	No, my friends aren't Canadian.
8. Do you have a brother?	*Yes, I have a brother. / No, I don't have a brother.*
9. Do you have my <u>dog</u>? (object pronoun)	*Yes, I have it. / No, I don't have it.*
10. Do you have some birds? (no)	*No, I don't have any birds.*

ANSWERS TO THE MID-TERM TEST 5 QUESTIONS

11.   Raymond is *<u>in front of</u>* the house.

12.   Nancy is *<u>at</u>* / *<u>in</u>* the window.

13.   One tree is *<u>in front of</u>* the apartments.

14.   Toto is *<u>beside</u>* / *<u>in front of</u>* Raymond.

15.   The number 11 is *<u>on</u>* the door.

16.   Ming lives *<u>at</u>* 13 Kent Street.

17.   Nancy lives *<u>on</u>* the third floor.

18.   Raymond is *<u>beside / behind</u>* Toto.

19.   Nancy lives *<u>on</u>* Kent Street.

20.   Ming lives *<u>in</u>* a house.

21.   *Yes, I live on the fifth floor. / No, I don't live on the fifth floor.*

22.   *My textbook is on my desk.*

23.   *There are _____ students here.*

24.   *There are _____ desks in this room.*

25.   *I am from _____.*

26.   *Yes, I have a sister. / No, I don't have a sister.*

27.   *Yes, I live in an apartment. / No, I don't live in an apartment.*

28.   *No, my dog is not under my desk. / No, my dog isn't under my desk.*

WAITER: (He asks Craig.)	Is the coffee yours?
CRAIG:	No, it's *<u>Jessica's</u>*. The tea is *<u>mine</u>*.
WAITER: (He asks Ruth and Carol.)	Is the Sprite yours?
RUTH AND CAROL:	No, it's *<u>Raymond and Tom's</u>*.
	The mango juice is *<u>ours</u>*.

NAME: _____

Answer the questions in sentences. (1-10, 5 marks each)

1. _____

2. _____

3. _____

4. _____

5. _____

6. _____

7. _____

8. _____

9. _____

10. _____

LESSON 20 CONTINUED

MID TERM TEST 5   NAME: _____

Use these prepositions to complete the sentences: (1 mark each)

in,   in front of,   on,   with,   at,   beside,   between

11. Raymond is _____ the house.

12. Nancy is _____ the window.

13. One tree is _____ the apartments.

14. Toto is _____ Raymond.

15. The number 11 is _____ the door.

16. Ming lives _____ 13 Kent Street.

17. Nancy lives _____ the third floor.

18. Raymond is _____ Toto.

19. Nancy lives _____ Kent Street.

20. Ming lives _____ a house.

Answer in sentences: (4 marks each)

21.   Do you live on the fifth floor?

_____

22.   Where is your textbook?

_____

23.   How many students are here?

_____

MID TERM TEST   NAME: _____

24. How many desks are in this room?

_____

25. Where are you from?

_____

26. Do you have a sister?

_____

27. Do you live in an apartment?

_____

28. Is your dog under your desk?

_____

Some friends are in a restaurant.
Jessica orders coffee.
Craig orders tea.
Raymond and Tom order Sprite.
Ruth and Carol order mango juice.

Craig   Jessica   Ruth   Carol   Raymond   Tom

Complete their answers using:
mine, yours, his, hers, ours, yours, theirs   (2 marks each)

WAITER: (He asks Craig.)   Is the coffee yours?

CRAIG: No, it's _____.

                                            The tea is _____.

WAITER: (He asks Ruth and Carol.)   Is the Sprite yours?

RUTH AND CAROL: No, it's _____.

                                            The mango juice is _____.

Teacher Guide

Teacher Guide

Image Credits

Teacher Guide

Visit us Online for More

https://www.efl-esl.com

BEGINNERS ESL LESSON PLANS BOOK 1

BEGINNERS LESSON PLANS BOOK 1

**20 complete lesson plans
3 Textbooks plus
Downloadable Audio and
Video**

Includes:

- Student Reader
- Student Workbook
- Teachers Guide
- 20 lessons
- 5 tests
- 4 reviews
- Glossary
- Download PDF or Paperback

Book 1 Overview

BEGINNERS ESL LESSON PLANS BOOK 2

BEGINNERS LESSON PLANS BOOK 2

**20 complete lesson plans
3 Textbooks plus
Downloadable Audio and
Video**

Includes:

- Student Reader
- Student Workbook
- Teachers Guide
- 20 lessons
- 5 tests
- 4 reviews
- Glossary
- Download PDF or Paperback

Book 2 Overview

Teach Your Students Online

You provide the Students
We provide the curriculum and platform

- Level 1 Beginners – Book 1 now available
- Teachers – FREE
- Students – $19.99/month
- Our commission – 30%
- Fully Customizable

https://teacher.efl-esl.com

Online ESL Teaching Platforms – The Complete Guide

Learn:

- Challenges of online teaching
- Certification Options
- What to look for in an online ESL teaching platform
- Tips for online promotion

https://efl-esl.com/teach-your-students-online/

High Beginners ESL Book 1

includes 3 Textbooks plus video and audio

- Full Audio and Video
- Complete Lesson Plans ready for the classroom
- Student Reader
- Student Workbook
- Teachers Guide
- 20 lessons
- 5 tests
- 4 reviews
- Glossary
- Download PDF or paperback

Book 1 Overview

High Beginners ESL Book 2

includes 3 Textbooks plus video and audio

- Full audio and video
- Student Reader
- Student Workbook
- Teacher's Guide
- 20 lessons
- 5 tests
- 2 review lessons
- Glossary
- PDF Format Download
- Download PDF or Paperback

Book 2 Overview

Beginners ESL Video Workbook

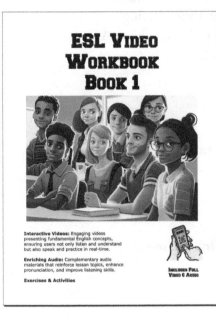

innovative ESL Video Workbook designed especially for beginners learning English as a second language! This comprehensive toolkit integrates:

Interactive Videos: Engaging videos presenting fundamental English concepts, ensuring users not only listen and understand but also speak and practice in real-time.

Enriching Audio: Complementary audio materials that reinforce lesson topics, enhance pronunciation, and improve listening skills.

Exercises & Activities: A variety of exercises including:

- **Role Plays:** Develop conversational skills through real-life scenarios.
- **Match the Meaning:** Connect words with their respective meanings to build vocabulary.
- **Fill in the Blank:** Improve grammar and context understanding by completing sentences.
- **Question and Answer:** Boost comprehension through interactive Q&A sessions.

Learn More https://efl-esl.com/video-workbooks/

Listening and Speaking Workbook

Complete Listening and Speaking English Workbook – includes full downloadable audio!

- Vocabulary for each Lesson
- Everyday Conversations – Listen to full audio then role-play!
- 14 Lessons
- 2 Review Chapters
- 2 Full Audio Tests with Answer Key
- Role Play
- Telephone Conversations and role play
- Question and Answer Dialogues

https://efl-esl.com/listening-speaking-english/

The History of Flight
Intermediate to Advanced ESL Lesson plans

20 ESL Lesson Plans for Intermediate to Advanced Students

Includes:

- Full downloadable Audio
- Student Worksheets
- Teacher Guide
- Student Reader
- Student Workbook
- Teacher Guide

Learning English
Curriculum
Since 1999
www.efl-esl.com

Includes Full Audio

Intermediate to Advanced ESL Lesson Plans for Adults
From the Ancient Greeks to Leonardo Da Vinci's flying machines, to Orville and Wilbur Wright, to WWII flying Ace, the Red Baron, to modern day space travel!

Includes:

- **Full audio**
- 20 Lessons – 40 hours of classroom time!
- Print as many Copies as Required!
- Teacher's guide
- Student Reader
- Student Workbook
- Complete instructions — ready for the classroom
- No preparation

https://efl-esl.com/curriculum/flight/

Children's ESL

This book introduces the alphabet from A to L and the numbers from 1 – 10.

Includes:

- Student book – 37 pages
- Student Workbook – 24 pages
- Teacher's Guide Book – 50 pages
- Glossary — 142 new words
- Colorful games and activities suitable for lamination –use over and over!

https://efl-esl.com/alphabet-activities-for-esl-students/

ESL Graphic Novels for Kids (Comic Books)

These books offer an oral approach for young ESL / EFL students aged 6 - 10.

They contain high interest stories, written in the graphics novel format that children love. This is very suitable for supplementary study, home school, as well as for summer camps.

https://efl-esl.com/esl-graphic-novels-for-children/

Made in the USA
Monee, IL
08 March 2024

54673713R00105